DATE DUE

DEC 18 1992	3/24/16
MAR 21 1995	MAY 15 2016
MAR 20 1995	
DEC 09 1996	
DEC 13 1996	
MAR 17 1997	
MAY 27 1997	
OCT 13 1997	
NOV 19 1997	
OCT 21 1998	
FEB 26 2004	
May 29, 2012	
MAY 12 2013	
april 30, 2014	

TWAYNE'S UNITED STATES AUTHORS SERIES

Emily Dickinson

TUSAS 280

Emily Dickinson

EMILY DICKINSON

By PAUL J. FERLAZZO

Michigan State University

TWAYNE PUBLISHERS

A DIVISION OF G. K. HALL & CO., BOSTON

Library of Congress Cataloging in Publication Data

Ferlazzo, Paul J.
Emily Dickinson.

(Twayne's United States authors series: TUSAS 280)
Bibliography: p. 157
Includes index.
1. Dickinson, Emily, 1830–1886. 2. Poets, American—19th century—Biography.
PS1541.Z5F4 811'.4 [B] 76–48304
ISBN 0-8057-7180-8 (Hardcover)
ISBN 0-8057-7425-4 (Paperback)
First Paperback Edition, March 1984

MANUFACTURED IN THE UNITED STATES OF AMERICA

To
Carole

Contents

About the Author

Paul J. Ferlazzo, after receiving his B.A. in English from St. Francis College in 1966, was awarded an NDEA Fellowship for graduate study at the University of Oklahoma, from which he obtained his M.A. in 1967, and Ph.D. in 1970. He is professor of English and department chairman at Montana State University.

Professor Ferlazzo's publications include critical articles on Whitman, Thoreau, Dickinson, Sandburg, popular culture, and regionalism. He is also the editor of *Critical Essays on Emily Dickinson.*

While teaching at Michigan State University he earned a Teacher-Scholar Award in 1974, and a Fulbright Lectureship in American literature at the University of Bologna, 1975–76. He is presently a vice-president of the Fulbright Alumni Association.

Preface

Writing an introductory study to Emily Dickinson's life and work in a single slender volume is getting more and more difficult to do. The quantity of excellent research and scholarship about her that must be considered is extremely large, and it is growing larger every year. The most difficult tasks a writer faces are those which require him to choose what seem to be major areas of study and to find an organization which allows for their clearest presentation. To accomplish these objectives, I have limited myself to what seemed like the most direct approach. After the first chapter, which counters the "myth of Emily" with the known data of her life, five thematic chapters follow which weave ample commentaries of her poetry with discussions of the era in which she lived, the influences and forces which contributed to the formation of her mind, and her own unique tendencies of feeling and perception. The seventh chapter treats her prose not only as an often-ignored form of her art but also as material that reveals other sides of her life and personality. The final chapter considers her influence upon modern writing.

In writing this book, I have accrued an indebtedness to so many. First, to my friend and colleague, an exemplary scholar of highest merit, David D. Anderson, whose faith in me and continual encouragement has been a wellspring of strength, I offer my most heartfelt thanks. To the fine scholars and writers whose works have helped to develop and affirm my own convictions, and served as guides through the high tricky passes of Emily Dickinson's thought, I salute them and send them my gratitude. A special tribute needs to be paid to these half-dozen out of the many—Charles R. Anderson, Richard Chase, John Cody, Clark Griffith, Thomas H. Johnson, and Richard B. Sewall. And to my wife, who in countless ways made it possible, I dedicate this book.

Quotations from *The Poems of Emily Dickinson*, edited by Thomas H. Johnson and *The Letters of Emily Dickinson*, edited by Thomas H. Johnson and Theodora V. Ward, are reprinted by permission of the Trustees of Amherst College. Permission to quote from the latter volume has also been obtained from the Harvard

University Press. An earlier version of the closing section of Chapter 3 appeared in *The Emily Dickinson Bulletin*.

PAUL J. FERLAZZO

Michigan State University

Chronology

1830 Emily Elizabeth Dickinson born December 10 in Amherst, Massachusetts.

1840 April, the family moves from the Homestead on Main Street to a house on North Pleasant Street. September 7, begins first year at Amherst Academy.

1846 Late August to mid-September, in Boston for her health.

1847 August 10, finishes her seventh year at Amherst Academy. September 30, enters Mount Holyoke Female Seminary in South Hadley.

1848 January, Emily undergoes a severe religious crisis. August, ends one-year stay at Mount Holyoke. Meets Benjamin F. Newton.

1850 January, Newton sends Emerson's *Poems* to Emily. November 30, Leonard Humphrey, one of her first "masters," dies.

1852 February 20, mock valentine, "Sic transit," published in the *Springfield Republican.*

1853 March 24, Ben Newton dies in Worcester.

1855 March, meets Reverend Charles Wadsworth in Philadelphia. November, the family moves back to the old house on Main Street. Mother's long illness begins.

1858 Forms a friendship with Samuel Bowles, the editor of the *Springfield Republican.* First "Master" letter drafted, addressed to someone she loves.

1860 Mid-March, Reverend Charles Wadsworth visits Emily in Amherst.

1861 Drafts second "Master" letter. May 4, "I taste a liquor never brewed" printed in the *Springfield Republican.*

1862 Winter, Emily suffers an emotional crisis. March 1, the *Springfield Republican* prints "Safe in their Alabaster Chambers." April 15, begins correspondence with Thomas Wentworth Higginson. Third "Master" letter drafted. She writes 366 poems during the year.

1864 March 12, *Round Table* prints "Some keep the Sabbath going to Church." March 30, the *Springfield Republican* prints "Blazing in gold, and quenching in purple." April to November, in Boston for eye treatments.

1865 April to October, again in Boston for eye treatments. End of her most prolific period.

1866 February 14, "A narrow fellow in the Grass" printed in the *Springfield Republican*.

1870 August 16, visit by Thomas W. Higginson.

1873 December 3, second and last visit by Higginson.

1874 June 16, father dies in Boston. Turns to Judge Otis P. Lord for consolation.

1875 June 15, mother stricken with paralysis; Emily becomes her constant attendant.

1878 January 16, Samuel Bowles dies. "Success is counted sweetest" published in an anonymous volume, *A Masque of Poets*. Relationship with Judge Lord blossoms into love after his wife's death in December, 1877.

1880 Early August, unexpected and final visit from Reverend Charles Wadsworth.

1882 April 1, Reverend Wadsworth dies. Mother dies on November 14.

1883 October 5, deeply affected by death of her favorite nephew, Gilbert.

1884 March 13, Judge Lord dies. June 14, suffers first attack of her final illness.

1885 Ill during the fall and confined to bed.

1886 Emily Elizabeth Dickinson dies on May 15. Lavinia burns most of her sister's correspondence but saves the poetry.

1890 First edition of Emily's poetry published, edited by a neighbor, Mabel Loomis Todd, and Thomas W. Higginson.

CHAPTER 1

Legend and Life

THE image of Emily Dickinson for many people has been a sensational mixture of sentiment and romance, but her most popular portrayal has been that of the "New England Nun." In this version of her life we see an heroic virgin who, in white, cloistered behind the walls of her father's house, renounced the world in order to nurture in sorrow the higher, purer love of one forever absent. In the silence of her cell, our heroine opens her heart in prayerful release to pent-up emotion by writing little terse poems to the mysterious missing lover. While thwarted love has been the central fact of the legend about her, her sympathetic attachment to nature and to children has enhanced its sentimentality. Shy and painful in the company of men, she communes on a high spiritual level with God's little creatures—the bee, the bird, and the boy. Finally, at the time of her death, the discovery of a cache of letters and poems revealing the true extent of her talent and of her silent suffering in the cause of love confirms the heroic stature of the myth. Trapped by an era considered intellectually dogmatic and emotionally limited, the poet triumphs through her writing, which outlives the age and proves to be timeless. The poet enters the popular consciousness as a symbol of all natural but hidden genius, and of all the love that is denied freedom.

In these terms Emily Dickinson's life appeals to the youthful and to the romantic imaginations. Many students and casual readers of her poetry have enjoyed hearing tales about her which remind them of storybook heroines locked in castles, of beautiful maidens cruelly relegated to a life of drudgery and obscurity, of genius so great that all the world's suppression cannot deny its flowering. To them her life stands for immortality through love, the superiority of feeling and sensitivity over reason and order, and boundless optimism in the face of suffering. She appears, therefore, as the saintly representative of virtues and values that ordinary people may admire or fantasize about in their fiction and day dreams but lack the will or opportunity to realize for themselves.

I *The Creation of a Myth*

The responsibility for the creation and perpetuation of the "myth of Emily" can be traced to her earliest biographers and to the novelists and playwrights who have freely rendered an account of her life in semifictional forms. Martha Dickinson Bianchi, a niece of the poet, who began in 1914 issuing selections of the poetry from manuscripts in her possession, gave voice to the core of the legend by referring to Dickinson's hidden love life and to one particular tragic affair of the heart. In an introductory essay to *The Single Hound* (1914), she writes that "The list of those whom she bewitched . . . included college boys, tutors, law students, the brothers of her girl friends,—several times their affianced bridegrooms even; and then the maturer friendships,—literary, Platonic, Plutonic; passages varying in intensity, and at least one passionate attachment, whose tragedy was due to the integrity of the lovers, who scrupled to take their bliss at another's cost."[1]

In Bianchi's 1924 volume entitled *The Life and Letters of Emily Dickinson*, the chapter entitled "The End of Peace" continues the story of this "passionate attachment." Bianchi offers a brief but suggestive description of an overpowering love for an unnamed married man that Emily Dickinson met in Philadelphia in the spring of 1854. Because she could not violate the moral codes of her society and destroy the happy life of the man's wife, Dickinson withdrew completely, and forever, into the protection of her father's house. The man, unable to live with such sacrifice, withdrew with his family to the other side of the continent. Bianchi tantalized her readers by hinting at certain family secrets concerning the man and this affair—secrets which could never be disclosed now since Dickinson's family took her secrets with it to the grave. An intriguing though undocumented story, it contains just enough detail to make us wish for more.[2]

Two book-length biographies in 1930 attempted, like Bianchi's essays, to solve the mystery surrounding Dickinson's life, to give rational reasons for a life-style sometimes referred to as morbid or abnormal. However, with an undue emphasis on the love story as the central fact of her life, what both finally achieved was to romanticize and make even more remote and unexplainable the heart and the soul of Emily Dickinson. Each biographer introduced a candidate for the role of paramour and heaped a good deal of sentimentality on both men. To Josephine Pollitt in *Emily Dickinson: The Human Background of Her Poetry*, Major Edward B. Hunt, the first husband of Dickinson's childhood friend Helen Hunt Jackson, was the secret man in Dickinson's life.[3] According to Pollitt, Dickinson met Hunt, a handsome, brilliant engineering officer in the army, during her visit to Philadelphia in 1854. He was irresistibly drawn to Dickinson because, unlike his wife, who was a sensual distraction for him, Dickinson was an appreciative listener and had a keen inquiring mind. Pollitt imagines a number of conversations between the lovers which indicate that they were opposites—he, a rational scientist, she, an emotional artist—brought into an ideal harmony through their mutual understanding and attraction. But Dickinson gave him back to his wife; and, as a result of their hidden love, she was filled with the suffering and passion necessary for continued poetic creations. When Major Hunt died accidentally in October, 1863, during a military experiment, Pollitt takes as the final sign of Dickinson's enduring love the fact that she was immediately taken ill with nervousness, depression, and eye trouble, and that she eventually had to be sent to Boston seven months later for a physician's care.

Genevieve Taggard, whose biography *The Life and Mind of Emily Dickinson* was published six months after Pollitt's, proposed the name of George H. Gould as Dickinson's unknown lover.[4] She contended that Dickinson had probably fallen in love with Gould around 1850 when he was a student at Amherst College and a frequent visitor to the Dickinson household. After his graduation from Amherst and after additional study at the Union Seminary in New York City, Gould became a minister in Philadelphia where their love was rekindled in 1854 during Dickinson's visit to the city. Dickinson rejected him, Taggard maintains, because she could not leave her father who had grown too attached to her and jealous of her affections. As serious evidence to support her view, Taggard prints a sworn statement from a person identified only as "X" that testifies that three persons, including Dickinson's sister, Lavinia, told "X" that Gould was the man Dickinson loved.

These biographies are now considered inadequate for serious study of Emily Dickinson because their arguments were based on unfounded assumptions, on occasional hearsay, on coincidental occurences, and sometimes on erroneous evidence. However, they did succeed in the early years of Dickinson scholarship in creating the idea of a love story too delicious for the public to willingly surrender, and a heroized image of the poet which clouded the facts of the real woman was maintained. In fact, another early "biography" which tended to idealize and sentimentalize the poet was written by a man who had been born across the street from her in 1869. When MacGregor Jenkins recorded his childhood impressions of "Miss Emily" in *Emily Dickinson, Friend and Neighbor* in 1930,[5] his stated desire was to dispel myths concerning Dickinson and to make her appear more human and understandable.

Despite Jenkins's objectives and his recollections of her normal displays of affection toward children and friends, he includes in his book numerous instances where, perhaps unconsciously, his descriptions of her enhance her mysteriousness. We see a frail, ethereal figure floating through her garden who would unexplainably disappear at the sound of a footstep, or stare in a mystic trance at the sunset, or change her moods instantly and without apparent cause. Jenkins attributes her behavior to an extremely sensitive and poetic nature that dwelt most comfortably in the realm of the spirit. However sincere Jenkins's attempts at factual recollection were, we need to remember that a man sixty years of age was recalling a woman (whom he rarely saw), events, and feelings from a time some forty-five years earlier. Since nostalgia and sentimentality seem to lend quite naturally an inevitable coloration to his memories, Jenkins, instead of dispelling myths, aided in refining them.

Although these biographies were used by a limited though informed academic and professional audience (many of whom knew better), a much wider range of people were affected by the novels and plays which portray the poet in a similarly romanticized manner. These literary versions of her life consider the tragic love story to be the central fact of her life and imply that she withdrew from the world and became a poet because she could not have the man she loved. They share in common a fairly sentimental treatment of several other themes which have contributed to the legend about her: her acutely sensitive nature which affected the love of those around her, her affection for nature and children, and her hidden creative life. Although these plays and novels served to bring an obscure but great American writer to the public's attention, they also obscured for generations the truth about the real woman and poet who was Emily Dickinson.

Alison's House, a three-act play which earned Susan Glaspell the Pulitzer Prize for 1931, was concerned with the question of whether the family of a deceased poet had the right to withhold manuscripts or information about a figure who belonged to the world. Although the setting is Iowa and although the family is named Stanhope, the play is admittedly based upon incidents from the life of Emily Dickinson and upon the subsequent decisions of her literary executors and descendants. The action of the play revolves around a leather case which contains some unpublished poems by the deceased poet, Alison, which her sister has unsuccessfully tried to destroy by fire. Defending her actions she exclaims, "I say she does not belong to the world! I say she belongs to us. And I'll keep her from the world—I'll keep the world from getting her—if it kills me—and kills you all!"[6] When the poet's brother becomes aware of the content of these poems—the poet's undying love for a married Harvard English teacher, he agrees that the poems should be destroyed.

But the young niece of Alison prevails upon her father to preserve the poems and entrust them to her. She intends to give them to the world in the name of love: "It's here—the story she never told. She had written it, as it was never written before. The love that never died—loneliness that never died—anguish and beauty of her love!"[7] The play is primarily an encomium to the "spirit" of Emily Dickinson, and both the characters and audience are made to feel the influential presence of a great personality. As one character states, "She isn't dead. Anything about her is alive."[8] Her love for life and nature echo in the family's reminiscences of her, and they wonder why something from her didn't make something better of them.

In *Eastward in Eden*, a three-act play by Dorothy Gardner produced in 1947, the subject is the "love affair" between Dickinson and Reverend Charles Wadsworth. When Gardner imagines conversations between the lovers, she places in their mouths idealistic though sometimes confusing commentary about themselves. For instance, Dickinson defines love for Wadsworth in act 1, scene 2, in the following terms: "Love should be—*(Rapturously and passionately)*—Love should be all Being, every flower, all color, all sound, all earth and sky, all life *(Pause)*, and Death."[9] What this declaration means exactly no one can be sure, but Gardner's aim is obviously not to inform us about Emily Dickinson's feelings or ideas, but to suggest that they were extravagant and superior.

Frequently, in place of realistic dialogue, Gardner has Dickinson speak exact lines from her poems or paraphrases of them. This distracting effect tends to minimize the power of the ideas expressed in the whole poems by suggesting that they can be reduced to a sententious collection of mismatched phrases. We also sense that Gardner is resorting to theatricality because of the failure of her imagination to render in viable speech the character of the poet:

> Water is taught by thirst—transport by pain. Unless we know despair, how can we rise above it? We learn valor in the dark. Anguish makes us know death a little ahead of time, so we can tell others not to be afraid. I had one taste of life and it cost me exactly—an existence—but it taught me Eternity. Love is before life and after life, and when we love, earth is a part of heaven. That is what I believe—*but* without the loved one Eternity's wide pocket will be picked! I have faith but I want *proof.*[10]

There is an ambitious dream sequence in act 2, scene 3, in which Dickinson imagines married life with Wadsworth. In this scene she is sewing while he reads aloud from the book of poems *My Letters to the World* by an unnamed author. After reading a few poems from the book, Wadsworth realizes that the poems in this book must have been written by Emily herself. " 'You wrote—this—Letter to the World,' he realizes, and softly she replies, 'You are my world!' "[11]

Doubtless, a sensational story of star-crossed lovers makes a better drama than the story about a single, lonely girl who is writing poems in her room; but, by treating the creative life of Dickinson in such a shallow manner, Gardner distorted the portrayal of the woman who was above all else a great poet. Gardner, who was begging for our sympathy for a broken heart rather than calling forth our admiration of genius, succeeded in reducing the great interior life of the poet to an adolescent fantasy.

Other falsification in the play not only violates our appreciation of Dickinson as an artist but damages the role of Charles Wadsworth. The most reliable biographer at the time of the writing of this play, George Frisbie Whicher, acknowledges the fact that Wadsworth was "a friend of supreme importance in Emily Dickinson's life." But, in the absence of evidence, he argues that we should not assume "that she was of supreme importance in his."[12] Whicher never refers to Wadsworth as her lover; based on an analysis of his character, that role would have been impossible for him to play. Gardner took liberties with Wadsworth's character, it would seem, in an attempt to create a romantic image for Dickinson which had no basis in fact, and which, indeed, stood in sharp contrast to the known facts.

The last play we should consider, *Come Slowly Eden* by Norman Rosten, is perhaps less guilty of the sentimental excesses found in the plays by Gardner and Glaspell; but it does maintain the image of Emily Dickinson as the enigmatic, ethereal creature whose poems sprang from mysterious wells of passion and experience. Colonel Thomas W. Higginson, acting as the narrator and the literary executor within the story, states early the objective of the play: "How to find a way toward her real life through these poems? No dates, no titles, merely clues. We shall have to guess at many things. We shall step lightly through her days, her gardens, her dawns and evenings, clouds, storm and pain. And more passion than I had imagined."[13] The play is cast in the form of a mystery with the poetry and letters as evidence of character and with Higginson and Dickinson's sister, Lavinia, as witnesses.

Despite its intended critical approach, the play remains largely a showcase for the recital of some forty of Dickinson's most popular poems, as well as numerous passages from her letters which hint at her sensitivity, loneliness, and love. There is a token effort early in the play to explore the poet's technique when Higginson recites "A route of evanescence" and concludes, "Dear me, we're still in the Nineteenth Century, but *she* is somewhere ahead! Two Lines rhymed in eight . . . what will they make of it later on?"[14] Occasionally, poems are fitted into the action, as when Emily explains to her father and sister why she missed breakfast by reciting "A bird came down the walk." However, most of the poems and letters are given a biographical reading. For instance, "Going to heaven!" and "Some keep the Sabbath going to church" are meant to summarize her religious opinions. All of act 2 is devoted to the love poetry with the intention of fitting the poems into her meetings with Reverend Wadsworth. For example, "If you were coming in the fall" is meant to describe her five-year wait to see him after their first meeting.

The unreliability of the play lies in its assumption that direct correspondences can and should be made between literal facts regarding the poet's life and her imaginative expressions in poetry. Whether or not such correlations ought to be made in the case of a private poet like Dickinson is a highly debatable issue. Rosten's tendency is to "fill in" certain partially documented facts with notions and feelings expressed in the poetry. Not only is the method unsound, but the results produce an image of the poet dominated by unclear data and often mysterious or simplistic characterizations.

Two novels might be briefly described for their contributions to the false and idealistic image of Emily Dickinson. The first, *Emily* by MacGregor Jenkins, is a novelistic version of his nostalgic biography *Emily Dickinson, Friend and Neighbor;* and it portrays Dickinson as the same remote, unearthly creature of feeling and perception. However, in the novel he takes liberties with dates in the family chronology; and he creates imaginary characters and events which act as setting and props for playing out what Jenkins calls "the controlling influences of her life and experience."[15]

In the second novel, *Come Slowly Eden*, Laura Benet humbly claimed not to be writing a biographical study but only "a fictional account of certain scenes and episodes in her life as I have imagined them, and without any intention to distort the personality of any of the characters."[16] Although she claimed a stronger attachment to the truth than Jenkins, she succeeded in creating a melodramatic love story worthy of the romance magazine. As a young girl, Dickinson is portrayed as beautiful, vivacious, witty, and better at doing everything young girls do than any of her friends or cousins. She is also kind and sensitive, and she speaks in breathless and profound sentences to her contemporaries. Her elders are charmed by her clever observations and are willingly confounded by her prankish airs. Poems "beat in her brain," and she playfully tosses them off before retiring. All the young men are in love with her, and by halfway through the book kisses are stolen from her and two ardent men have proposed marriage.

The fanciful behavior of youth ends when she meets Reverend Wadsworth in Philadelphia in 1854. She falls hopelessly in love with him at first sight, and he with her, and both suffer dearly for it since he is already married. Their meetings are filled with tears and exclamations of soul-uniting love. Their last meeting is classic for its extravagantly emotional farewell scene:

At sight of her tears he rose and stood before her. Then, suddenly lifting her, he took her to him, held her close, pressed his lips hard upon hers: "I must have you with me," he whispered passionately. . . .

And as he turned his head to gaze imploringly and wildly at her. Emily felt the very nerves and sinews of her body rent and torn. If all the blood had flowed from her heart in that instant, she would not have known surprise. . . .

"Ah," she cried hungrily, "hush! But please say that one word again—just to me—one word! I can perish then!"

"No. Nothing must happen to *you!*" he cried in agony. . . .

Emily found herself conscious once more. "If I *could*," she breathed in answer, "but you are another woman's destiny. Your wife. What if I were in her place?"

"I know," he groaned, "but you and I are one in spirit and in the truth."

She held his head against her breast that throbbed as with a mortal wound.[17]

The action of the novel is so overdrawn that it is unreliable for its insights into character and motivation. There is an overwhelming sense that Laura Benet tried to fit the life of Dickinson into a prefabricated story form which would appeal to a mass audience. Although it remains faithful to names, dates, and actual events, Benet's novel suffers from an obvious intention to propagate the image of Emily Dickinson as romantic heroine.

The mythical Emily Dickinson reflected in popular literature and in the early biographies may be as enduring as the real one. However, since 1939 and the publication of the first authoritative biography, *This Was a Poet* by George F. Whicher, scholarly and academic study of the poet has revealed that the real woman and poet may prove to be more interesting than the myth—and certainly more important.

II *Amherst*

Emily Dickinson was born on December 10, 1830, in Amherst, Massachusetts, a small Connecticut River Valley farming community with a population somewhat less than three-thousand. The town had deep roots in Calvinist doctrine dating back six generations to the period from 1672 to 1729 when "Pope" Solomon Stoddard ruled the whole Hampshire district with autocratic power. The emotionalism stirred by his revival harvests, along with the stern orthodoxy of his successor, his grandson Jonathan Edwards, helped to form a staunch Puritan culture in the Valley's little villages. As for the churches in Amherst at the time of Dickinson's birth, they were orthodox Congregational with services attended twice on Sundays and with daily Bible reading encouraged at home. Sermons stressed man's depravity, the necessity of conversion, the imminence of death, and God's wrath. Although Emily Dickinson rejected the mournful dogmas of Calvinism, she lived in a community preoccupied with Calvinist eschatology. Her own compulsive interest in death (almost a third of her poems deal with the subject), as well as her numerous poems on the religious experience and God, reveal her inescapable heritage.

Public responsibility, self-descipline, and moral sensitivity were virtues the town revered. Almost every family grew its own necessary fruit and vegetables on its own land, and raised enough livestock to supply the family with eggs, cheese, and salt pork. The people of Amherst lived by the time-honored New England practices of thrift, industry, and moderation. Although Puritan attitudes toward pleasure and entertainment were indeed prevalent in Amherst, the men were too engaged in business affairs and the women were too busy with the heavy routine of housekeeping for them to enjoy a generous amount of relaxation and amusement. Card games, dancing, and novel reading, while enjoyed in nearby larger towns, were prohibited in the Amherst of 1830. Social activity was largely limited to evening visits among neighbors and to informal suppers. The August commencement exercises at Amherst College and the October cattle show were the two major social events of the year.

However, this simple social life of Emily Dickinson's younger years gave way to a more sophisticated life by the 1860s—about the time she was withdrawing from the world. Increased wealth and comforts, as well as broader communication with the outside world, led to a greater interest in the cultivation of social graces. Dickinson's sister-in-law, Sue, who, lived in the house next door became, in fact, one of the bright lights of this changing scene.

The town's evangelical Puritanism had remained uniform for nearly a century when Amherst College was founded in 1821 to perpetuate orthodoxy against the onslaught of Unitarianism issuing from Harvard. The heretical threats of Harvard were a concern to all the Congregational churches in western Massachusetts and Connecticut, and they eagerly supported the infant college. In hindsight, as George Frisbie Whicher has noted, Emily Dickinson and Amherst College share much in common.[18] Her grandfather, Samuel Fowler Dickinson, was its most active founder; and, between her father and her brother, they held the office of college treasurer for sixty years. But, beyond these facts, both college and poet were conceived and raised in Puritan orthodoxy, only to develop liberal spirits that turned away from inherited beliefs through a desire to understand and appreciate the larger world around them.

III *Family Portraits*

Emily Dickinson's was the eighth generation of a family that had lived and prospered in New England since the great Puritan migration of the seventeenth century. The redbrick mansion in which she was born and lived most of her life was the proud work of her grandfather, and it stood as a monumental symbol of the stature and achievement of the Dickinson family. The household was secure and well-ordered, dominated as it was by her father, Edward Dickinson. A lawyer with a thriving practice, he had served his community throughout his lifetime in a number of responsible positions. He had been the treasurer of Amherst College for nearly forty years; he had served numerous times as a state legislator and once as a United States Congressman; he was involved in numerous local community projects of importance. He helped to bring the railroad to Amherst, encouraged the establishment of Episcopal and Catholic churches, and subscribed to many private charities. He exhibited the best qualities of the Whig gentleman and was every bit a leading citizen of trustworthy judgment and reliable vigorous action.

Edward Dickinson's letter, written as a young man to his future wife, aptly describes the all-encompassing, rigid sense of duty which characterized the life of the man: "May blessings rest upon us, and wake us happy—May we be virtuous, intelligent, industrious and by the exercise of every virtue, & the cultivation of every excellence, be esteemed & respected & beloved by all—We must determine to do our duty to each other, & to all our friends, and let others do as they may."[19] Despite his stress upon virtue and duty, displays of affection and enthusiasm were not impossible for him; but such displays were rare. Two anecdotes describing his spontaneity have been remembered and recorded probably because they were remarkably out of keeping with his usually stern behavior. One afternoon in September, 1851, he rang the bell of the Baptist Church to alert the townspeople to a particularly beautiful sunset; and in April, 1874, he rushed outdoors in slippers to feed a small group of hungry birds in the springtime snow.

His affect upon his daughter, Emily, was enormous. As Whicher describes it, "His gods were her gods."[20] She stood in awe of him as a child, and she anticipated his will as a grown woman. His death in June, 1874, sealed her seclusion. In July, she wrote to Higginson: "His heart was pure and terrible and I think no other like it exists."[21] As for Emily Dickinson's mother, she did not have as much importance for her. In a rather cruel way, Dickinson told Colonel Higginson, "I never had a mother. I suppose a mother is one to whom you hurry when you are troubled."[22]

Emily Norcross had attended a finishing school for young ladies in New Haven; she appears to have been a submissive, gentle woman who was drawn instinctively to the intense masculinity of Edward Dickinson; and they were married on May 7, 1828. She was devoted to her husband and understood her role to be one in which she simply served her husband and maintained a well-ordered home for him. A year after her husband's death, Mrs. Dickinson became paralyzed and remained an invalid for seven years, largely under the care of her daughter, Emily; and not until this time did her daughter begin to accept and cherish her.[23]

Emily had a close and understanding relationship with her older brother, Austin, who was born April 16, 1829. Although he possessed his father's integrity and sagacity in practical affairs, he was temperamentally very different. In place of the grave and solid manner of his father, Austin was humorous, outspoken, and appreciated beauty and art. His youthful desire to move to a western city was altered by his father's persuasion to remain in Amherst and to follow to some degree in his own footsteps. After attending Amherst College and Harvard Law School, Austin became his father's law partner, lived next door to the Dickinson mansion, and eventually succeeded his father as treasurer of the college. His energies, like his father's, were directed toward the community. He organized a Village Improvement Association, founded and directed banks and public utilities, supervised the building of a new church, and served as moderator of the town meetings for twenty years.

Austin's wife, the former Sue Gilbert, had been a schoolmate of Emily's at Amherst Academy. She was intelligent and witty, and openly delighted in the gaiety and in the conversations at the lavish dinner parties that she loved to host. Her entertainments were lively and usually attended by distinguished company. One guest penetrated beneath her glittering charm and left this portrait which touches the complexity of her character:

> The social leader of the town was Mrs. Austin Dickinson, a really brilliant and highly cultivated woman of great taste and refinement, perhaps a little too aggressive, a little too sharp in wit and repartee, and a little too ambitious for social prestige, but, withal, a woman of the world in the best sense, having a very keen and correct appreciation of what was fine and admirable. Her imagination was exceedingly vivid, sometimes so vivid that it got away with her and she confounded its pictures with objective things. If she had had sufficient application, she would have rivaled Cervantes as a writer of romance and adventure. . . . Mrs. Dickinson was, I suppose, by descent a Puritan, but she was not much of a Puritan in her mentality.[24]

Emily accepted Sue for many years as a sister, trusted friend, and showed her over three hundred poems. But Sue violated Emily's trust when she allowed one of her poems to be printed in *The Springfield Republican* in 1866. A strain developed between the two which magnified other differences; and as they gradually drifted apart, they maintained merely perfunctory relationships.

Lavinia, Emily's young sister, born on February 28, 1833, was an aggressive, practical woman who was forthright in manner and blunt in speech. Without the emotional crisis or creativity of her sister Emily, Vinnie quietly remained at home, never married, and helped to maintain the household. Devoted to Emily, she spent her life protecting her sister's privacy and sharing her confidences. After Emily died, Vinnie was in the process of carrying out her sister's final request to burn her papers when she discovered bundles of poems; and her faith in the worth of what her adored sister had written led to their eventual publication.

IV *Friendships and Affections*

While Emily Dickinson was at Amherst Academy, she maintained the close friendship of several young girls, especially Abiah Root, Abby Wood, and Jane Humphrey. These friendships lasted into early maturity and were kept lively through correspondence until marriage and travel away from Amherst brought their relationships to a natural close. During her last term at the Academy, Dickinson came under the influence of the young principal, Leonard Humphrey. He was a former Amherst College valedictorian, a friend of Austin, and a member of the same fraternity to which Austin belonged. Although it is probable he regarded Emily Dickinson as nothing more than a bright student, her comments after his sudden death in 1850 reveal that she somewhat idolized him and considered him as one of her first "masters." To Abiah Root, she wrote:

> I write Abiah to-night, because it is cool and quiet, and I can forget the toil and care of the feverish day, and then I am *selfish* too, because I am feeling lonely; some of my friends are gone, and some of my friends are sleeping—sleeping the churchyard sleep—the hour of evening is sad—it was once my study hour—my master has gone to rest, and the open leaf of the book, and the scholar at school *alone*, make the tears come, and I cannot brush them away; I would not if I could, for they are the only tribute I can pay the departed Humphrey.
>
> *You* have stood by the grave before; I have walked there sweet summer evenings and read the names on the stones, and wondered who would come and give me the same memorial; but I never have laid my friends there, and forgot that they too must die; this is my first affliction, and indeed 'tis hard to bear it. (*L*, I, 102–3)

While she was attending Mt. Holyoke Seminary, the twenty-seven-year-old Benjamin F. Newton arrived in Amherst for a two-year apprenticeship in her father's law firm before beginning his own practice in Worcester. Newton was a Unitarian, something of an advanced thinker, and evidently aware of contemporary literature. As his and Emily's friendship developed, Newton exposed her to the world of thought and writing from which she had been sheltered. According to tradition, he gave her Lydia Child's socially radical book, *Letters from New York;* but his most important gift was a copy of Ralph Waldo Emerson's poems. From this book and from the later writings that she obtained of Emerson's, Dickinson found the liberating notion of self-reliance, the stress on personal experience over tradition, and the concept of poet as "seer"—all of which stirred her poetic ambitions and gave her the support and encouragement she needed to lead the rigorously lonely life she chose.

Not only did Newton show her intellectual and spiritual horizons that were beyond her limited experience, he also encouraged her in her writing and apparently told her she could become a great poet. After his death in 1853, when Dickinson wrote to Newton's minister in Worcester inquiring about his last hours, she acknowledged her great debt to him:

> Mr Newton was with my Father two years, before going to Worcester—in pursuing his studies, and was much in our family.
>
> I was then but a child, yet I was old enough to admire the strength, and grace, of an intellect far surpassing my own, and it taught me many lessons, for which I thank it humbly, now that it is gone. Mr Newton became to me a gentle, yet grave Preceptor, teaching me what to read, what authors to admire, what was most grand or beautiful in nature, and that sublimer lesson, a faith in things unseen, and in a life again, nobler, and much more blessed—
>
> Of all these things he spoke—he taught me of them all, earnestly, tenderly, and when he went from us, it was as an elder brother, loved indeed very much, and mourned, and remembered. (*L*, I, 282)

Her admiration and affection for Newton is clear from the letter, but anything approaching a romantic attachment to the young man is certainly absent. He was another early master, or "Preceptor," as she calls him; and he was one of the first, and few, to ever acknowledge her potential as a poet.

Among other young men who emerge as friends during her early years are George Gould, her brother's classmate and editor of the school paper which printed one of Dickinson's earliest prose valentines; Elbridge Bowdoin, her father's young law partner, to whom Dickinson once sent a mock-heroic valentine in thanks for lending her books; and Henry Emmons, a student at Amherst College with whom Dickinson went riding and exchanged flowers and books. All of these friendships were apparently playful and happy associations for Emily Dickinson, and they lacked any of the pressure or anxiety surrounding a romantic attachment or a secret passion.

V *Upbringing*

Emily's childhood was not so different from the early years of many New England girls of her period and station. She was reared to possess the graces, virtues, and abilities common to the nineteenth-century ideal of American womanhood. Her parents wished her to be a Christian, to attend to household duties, to enjoy in a limited way culture and education, and to devote herself someday to a husband of her own. However, her originality of soul, as we shall see later in this book, caused her to frustrate in later life every one of their expectations for her. In choosing to devote herself to the pursuit of great art, she challenged and rejected the psychic and social stereotyped images of the woman of her era.

She learned to play piano at a young age, and she was allowed to read books which, as her father put it, did not "joggle" her mind. Her education, while probably better than most Americans received at this time, was not of the quality offered to men of the period, whose minds were not nearly as great as hers; for her education was intended to prepare her for the roles she was expected to fulfill in later life. When she attended Amherst Academy from 1840 to 1847 on a fairly regular basis (but was withdrawn temporarily on account of an occasional illness), she received instruction in Latin, German, French, biology, geology, history, philosophy, and composition. She was a good student who liked her teachers and was liked and admired by them in return. She was so liked by her schoolmates for her wit and sincerity that a strong bond existed with several girls with whom she corresponded for many years.

Her final year of formal schooling was spent at Mount Holyoke Female Seminary (1847–1848), under the supervision of Mary Lyon, a pioneer in women's education. The school was well rated not only for its rigorous intellectual training but also for its close supervision of the students' religious activities—and Emily suffered a serious religious crisis. During the fall she attended special meetings for those who had not yet been converted, and she paid close attention to seminars and lectures stressing doom for the unrepentant. She considered carefully, searched her soul, and suffered much anguish, but finally reached a decision not to be converted. Her reasons are not completely known, but in a letter to her friend Abiah Root she expressed regret at not becoming a Christian, confiding that "it is hard for me to give up the world" (*L*, I, 67).

Emily began her adult life, therefore, with the conscience and the heart of a Christian but without the faith and the hopes that sustained other Christians when they were faced with the suffering and complexity of living. In refusing to "give up the world," she paradoxically withdrew from the world around her; and she began searching for another which she found, finally, in her own poetic creations.

CHAPTER 2

A Question of Faith

"COTTON Mather would have burnt her for a witch" concludes Allen Tate's famous essay about Emily Dickinson and her relation to the Puritan environment which surrounded her.[1] Although she never put a spell on anyone, conjured up the devil, or spoke to the dead, what was going on in her mind and in her poetry would have shocked her religiously devout forebears.

I *Religious Crisis*

She was reared in the Congregational Church; but, unlike her family, she never became a professed member of the church. Her greatest personal religious trials came as a young woman during her year at Mount Holyoke Seminary and for a few years following when the revival spirit was about in Amherst. Her letters from 1848 to 1854 reflect her struggles against the forces which challenged her to give herself openly to Christ. The letters move from hopeful consideration of church membership, through rebellion and fear of its outcome, to a resigned determination to stand apart from her community.

Her letter of January 17, 1848, to Abiah Root is filled with schoolgirl talk about Mount Holyoke and Thanksgiving vacation, and it closes with an optimistic self-appraisal concerning her church membership: "There is a great deal of religious interest here and many are flocking to the ark of safety. I have not yet given up to the claims of Christ, but trust I am not entirely thoughtless on so important & serious a subject" (*L*, I, 60). Yet, only four months later she writes to the same friend with almost complete panic how she feels herself to be lost:

> I tremble when I think how soon the weeks and days of this term will all have been spent, and my fate will be sealed, perhaps. I have neglected the *one thing needful* when all were obtaining it, and I may never, never again

pass through such a season as was granted us last winter. Abiah, you may be surprised to hear me speak as I do, knowing that I express no interest in the all-important subject, but I am not happy, and I regret that last term, when that golden opportunity was mine, that I did not give up and become a Christian. It is not now too late, so my friends tell me, so my offended conscience whispers, but it is hard for me to give up the world. I had quite a long talk with Abby while at home and I doubt not she will soon cast her burden on Christ. She is sober, and keenly sensitive on the subject, and she says she only desires to be good. How I wish I could say that with sincerity, but I fear I never can. *(L,* I, 67–68)

This revealing passage is filled with the emotional turmoil and the contradictions of a girl on the verge of maturity; she is trying to believe but is unable to do so; she recognizes that she should, but she feels that she cannot do so with sincerity. Her apparent reason centers on the phrase "it is hard for me to give up the world." Her experience of the world by this time had been very limited, of course, but she perceived better than most did that accepting New England orthodoxy meant shutting out forever the rich experience of new ideas and the joys of a world she had only glimpsed.

In her letters to friends in 1850, she continues to analyze her resistance to conformity and to express her aching fear that she may be lost forever. In April she writes to Jane Humphrey about the religious "harvest" occurring in Amherst and about how she feels a growing sense of isolation because of her rebellious attitude: "Christ is calling everyone here, all my companions have answered, even my darling Vinnie believes she loves, and trusts him, and I am standing alone in rebellion, and growing very careless. Abby, Mary, Jane, and farthest of all my Vinnie have been seeking, and they all believe they have found; I can't tell you *what* they have found, but *they* think it is something precious. I wonder if it *is?*" *(L,* I, 94).

Only one month later she feels confirmed in her wickedness and pictures herself to Abiah Root as a traitor or as a vagabond who is hiding her guilt from the eyes of worthy citizens: "[Abby] has told you about things here, how the 'still small voice' is calling, and how the people are listening, and believing, and truly obeying—how the place is very solemn, and sacred, and the bad ones slink away, and are sorrowful—not at their wicked lives—but at this strange time, great change. *I* am one of the lingering *bad* ones, and so do *I* slink away, and pause, and ponder, and ponder, and pause . . ." *(L,* I, 98). Finally, by the end of the year, she appears intoxicated with her spiritual wrecklessness and gallantly professes her independence:

"The shore is safer, Abiah, but I love to buffet the sea—I can count the bitter wrecks here in these pleasant waters, and hear the murmuring winds, but oh, I love the danger! You are learning control and firmness. Christ Jesus will love you more. I'm afraid he don't love me *any!*" (*L*, I, 104).

By 1854, Dickinson was ready to accept her "lost" condition and to live her life as she pleased with regard to religion. Sue Gilbert, her good friend and her brother's fiancé, was a devoted church member who had been pressuring both brother and sister into becoming members. Austin Dickinson eventually did so, but Emily sent this letter to Sue: "Sue—you can go or stay—There is but one alternative—We differ often lately, and this must be the last. . . . Sue—I have lived by this. It is the lingering emblem of the Heaven I once dreamed, and though if this is taken, I shall remain alone, and though in that last day, the Jesus Christ you love, remark he does not know me—there is a darker spirit will not disown it's [sic] child" (*L*, I, 305–6). She felt so strongly about her decision not to become a church member that she was evidently willing to forfeit an important and dear friendship with her future sister-in-law; perhaps, as she suggests in the last line, she is even willing to risk damnation.

She continued attending church services sporadically until the early 1860s when she withdrew entirely from the church and from the world. Since the Puritan church and Amherst society were so inextricably bound together, her struggle of more than a decade with the question of church membership amounted to a serious evaluation on her part of the whole spiritual and moral environment in which she found herself. Coextensive with the rejection of her church was the rejection of her society. As Allen Tate has argued in his essay about her relationship to New England culture, she perceived the decline of the old order and chose to withdraw to probe the deficiencies of the tradition and to make personal what was worthwhile in it, or to create what was lacking. Her position he calls the "perfect literary situation": she possessed the culture but was not confined within it.[2] However we may phrase her situation, the tensions in her mind that resulted from her struggle with orthodoxy have produced some of her finest poems.

II *Belief versus Disbelief*

Dickinson lived with doubt without ever despairing. She did not know the final answers to the important religious questions; and, what is more, she knew she could never know them. God, salvation, eternity, and sin were subjects which the ministers of her age and their devout followers had dealt with to their satisfaction but not to hers. Her attitude was not the result of her feeling intellectually superior to them; it was rather a matter of her perceiving the limitations of the human mind and of how it works to seek comforting and sometimes illusory assurances. Knowing these characteristics made her, in fact, humble; and, while it prevented her from self-confidently affirming her faith, it also preserved her from complete despair. If she did not *know* the truth, she did not deny that the truth might exist; and, as a result, it is possible to find in her poetry almost every aspect of doubt and belief about religious subjects. While she desired salvation and immortality, she denied the orthodox view of paradise; she wondered, in fact, if merely oblivion lay beyond the grave. Although she believed in a Creator, she sometimes doubted His benevolence. Sometimes in jest, sometimes in mockery she denies the Bible, sin, and orthodox piety. As with all subjects fit for meditation, she pursued eschatalogical questions with daring and perserverance wherever they might lead—to the bosom of the Father, or to the brink of cosmic annihilation. Since she permitted herself to experience the extremes of faith and of loss, her poetry records a great soul's journey to understand its place in the universe.

Dickinson's major poetic method in dealing with religious subjects reflects the tension in her mind between belief and disbelief. She begins a poem with a strong statement of faith, proceeds to examine it, qualify it, or question it, and then ends the poem with a statement of doubt or with one that indicates her condition of suspended judgement:

I know that He exists.
Somewhere—in Silence—
He has hid his rare life
From our gross eyes.

'Tis an instant's play.
'Tis a fond Ambush—
Just to make Bliss
Earn her own surprise!

But—should the play
Prove piercing earnest—

Should the glee—glaze—
In Death's—stiff—stare—

Would not the fun
Look too expensive!
Would not the jest—
Have crawled too far![3]

As one critic of the poem has described it, "The first line has the piety of heaven, the last the poison of hell."[4] Dickinson begins confidently with an orthodox statement that affirms that God exists and that He hides himself from us only to tease our love and to brighten our anticipation for Him. But, in the last two stanzas, she dramatically shifts her tone to one of worry over the final outcome of this hide-and-seek game that we play with a jesting God. If there is no salvation after death, she exclaims, a cruel joke indeed would have been played on us. The powerful last line suggests an evil sense of humor that is at play with its connotations of the serpentine or the monstrous.

This sense of worry about salvation after death takes many forms in every period of her life. In one later poem, this doubt solidifies into an almost prosaic statement of despair:

Those—dying then,
Knew where they went—
They went to God's Right Hand—
That Hand is amputated now
And God cannot be found—

(*P*, 1551; III, 1069)

She is nostalgic for the assurance that her Puritan forebears felt about life after death, and she is lamenting her generation's mutilation of doctrinal belief.

Another poem, one which begins in orthodoxy, distorts the conventional images of the afterlife to end in blatant skepticism:

Going to Heaven!
I don't know when—
Pray do not ask me how!
Indeed I'm too astonished
To think of answering you!
Going to Heaven!

How dim it sounds!
And yet it will be done
As sure as flocks go home at night
Unto the Shepherd's arm!

She continues in the second stanza by sardonically asking, "Perhaps you're going too!/Who knows?" Impishly, she requests that the "you" save her a place, for she will not take up much room or much glory. All she needs is the "smallest 'Robe' " and "just a bit of 'Crown'." Then she abruptly concludes:

I'm glad I don't believe it
For it w'd stop my breath—
And I'd like to look a little more
At such a curious Earth!
I'm glad they did believe it
Whom I have never found
Since the mightly Autumn afternoon
I left them in the ground.

(*P*, 79; I, 64)

She separates herself sharply from the conventionally faithful persons with the opposing predications, "I'm glad I don't . . . I'm glad they did." Contemplation of heaven for the faithful is reassuring; but for Dickinson, who loves this "curious Earth," it is an interference.

In another poem she separates herself more firmly from the doctrines and practices of organized religion after beginning with the resounding doctrinal assertion, "This World is not Conclusion." Her strategy in this poem is to expose the insubstantial intellectual content upon which faith in the afterlife is based:

This World is not Conclusion.
A Species stands beyond—
Invisible, as Music—
But positive, as Sound—
It beckons, and it baffles—
Philosophy—dont know—
And through a Riddle, at the last—
Sagacity, must go—
To guess it, puzzles scholars—
To gain it, Men have borne

Contempt of Generations
And Crucifixion, shown—
Faith slips—and laughs, and rallies—
Blushes, if any see—
Plucks at a twig of Evidence—
And asks a Vane, the way—
Much Gesture, from the Pulpit—
Strong Hallelujahs roll—
Narcotics cannot still the tooth
That nibbles at the soul—

(*P*, 501; II, 384–85)

The first stanza (there are five distinct quatrains although there are no spacings to indicate this) offers a feeling of finality, as if further discussion were unnecessary. But each succeeding stanza modifies its assertion until it is empty of all authority. The second and third stanzas eliminate philosophy, sagacity, and scholarship as knowledgeable or as trustworthy indicators of eternity. Philosophers do not know, sages must give way to the riddle of death, and scholars are simply puzzled. In the third stanza, she describes men of faith, martyrs, who have suffered contempt and even death for their belief. But faith is insufficient, we learn in the fourth stanza. Like a giddy drunkard, faith is awkward and weak: falling, laughing, and blushing, faith needs to clutch at twigs for support; and, like a person hopelessly lost in the fog of intoxication, faith is content to go in whichever direction the wind is blowing.

In the fifth stanza the church is depicted as theatrical, noisy, and essentially irrelevant. Rousing sermons and loud hymns, like a strong drug, may stupify the senses into submission; but they cannot ease the pain of gnawing doubt within her soul. The poem's grim ending reflects back to the beginning and adds an ironic dimension to the opening line: not to be found in this world is a conclusion of any sort. Everything about the human condition, Dickinson seems to be suggesting, is doubtful, contingent, and changing; and none of our intellectual or spiritual institutions offer, upon close inspection, a lasting peace of soul. Dickinson's is a modern vision of life, and we might be tempted to label it existentialist, yet, as Clark Griffith warns, such a label would be an "importation" where she is concerned.[5] Nevertheless, her frustrated search for certitude in a world that resisted giving it to her is part of what the modern reader finds of special interest in her work.

We also get a good idea in this poem of her intellectual independence: she resists pronouncements of authority; she resists truths based upon tradition or historicity. In some fourteen lines she discards as insufficient evidence the Christian spiritual and intellectual tradition about death and about salvation, and she upholds in its place the unresolved speculations of her own mind. In a similar mood at a later date, she playfully dismissed the greatest bulwark of authority, the Bible:

The Bible is an antique Volume—
Written by faded Men
At the suggestion of Holy Spectres—

(*P*, 1545; III, 1065)

"Antique" connotes something useless and outdated rather than rare and valuable. Just like other dull historical tomes, the Bible was written by pale men inspired by ghosts; they were not prophets inspired by God. Since the poem was originally sent to her nephew, Ned, with the title, "Diagnosis of the Bible, by a Boy," we should not accept it too literally or too seriously as some critics have. But the poem does reveal a consciousness that is unafraid to challenge and jest with sacred authority.

In another poem the orthodox notion that the dead are glorified in heaven is challenged by her perception of the vast distances between herself and the deceased:

Their Hight in Heaven comforts not—
Their Glory—nought to me—
'Twas best imperfect—as it was—
I'm finite—I cant see—

The House of Supposition—
The Glimmering Frontier that
skirts the Acres of Perhaps—
To me—shows insecure—

(*P*, 696; II, 537)

The symbolic landscape of the second stanza pictures heaven ("The House of Supposition") surrounded by "Acres of Perhaps" at a frontier so unclear and distant that she can never hope to be sure about it. She concludes the poem by emphasizing the lack of sufficient information and, therefore, her need for suspended judgement: "This timid life of Evidence/Keeps pleading—'I don't know.' " But she cannot be the complete skeptic, for in another poem in which answers are not forthcoming, she regrets her questioning intellect that will not settle for easy solutions; and she angrily wishes she had never been born:

'Twere better Charity
To leave me in the Atom's Tomb—
Merry, and Nought, and gay, and numb—
Than this smart Misery.

(*P*, 376; I, 299)

In Dickinson's iconoclastic tendencies, we can see her roots in Emerson. She had studied his essays and poetry, she owned at least a dozen of his books, her allusions to him in her letters and poems are third only to the Bible and to Shakespeare. As Hyatt Waggoner and Albert J. Gelpi have amply shown, Emerson's influence upon her gave her work its special quality, since she had read Emerson early in her mature years and since he had remained throughout her life a chief intellectual resource.[6] His stress on self-reliance and immediate personal experience over tradition should be apparent in the poems we have just discussed; but she owed much to Emerson in other ways. Her business as a poet, she told Higginson in her second letter to him, was "Circumference," an idea gleaned directly from Emerson's essay "Circles." His theory of "Compensation" is reflected in much of her writing, and her inconsistency and her reluctance to formulate a systematic philosophy finds support in the Emersonian principle of faithfulness to the person's deeper self. Although he served as a fountain of courage in her intellectual and spiritual experiments in searching for the truth, she could never break entirely as he did with the conventions which bound her. As Austin Warren has summarized her situation, "She is a rebel—but not, like Emerson, a schismatic."[7]

III *Safe in their Alabaster Chambers*

Appropriately, the final poem to be considered that demonstrates the strain in her mind between belief and disbelief is considered one of her greatest lyrics. The poem, "Safe in their Alabaster Chambers" (*P*, 216; I, 151–52), appears in two versions (1859 and 1861), in

Thomas H. Johnson's variorum edition; and we have reason to believe that Dickinson was unable to decide which version she preferred. Her indecision, the fact that she left both poems for us, reflects the unresolved tension she felt between the sense of faith present in the first version and the realization of cosmic indifference in the second.

The first stanzas of both versions are virtually identical:

> Safe in their Alabaster Chambers—
> Untouched by Morning
> And untouched by Noon—
> Sleep the meek members of the Resurrection—
> Rafter of satin,
> And Roof of stone.

In this stanza, we find an essentially religious view of death. Those waiting to be reborn are now safe in their graves, preserved from the movement and changes of time. They are also safe from sin in their cold, white, and sterile tombs of alabaster where they are untouched by the sensuous temptations of each day. They are meek in their expectations, for they realize that they are unworthy and that only through God's generosity will they be reborn. But we can discern here Dickinson's skill at subtly depicting the inconsistencies of human virtue. Since wealth in traditional Puritanism was a sign of God's elect, then these dead lying in coffins lined with satin will *surely* rise again.

The second stanza of the earlier version continues in a mood of promise and security:

> Light laughs the breeze
> In her Castle above them—
> Babbles the Bee in a stolid Ear,
> Pipe the Sweet Birds in ignorant cadence—
> Ah, what sagacity perished here!

The springtime images of the living world above the grave suggest that all is not lost. The breeze, the bee, and the birds give testament to the fact that life continues its endless cycle of renewal. But Dickinson also suggests a criticism of those who died, of those, she implies, who preferred death. The laughing breeze, the babbling bee, and the sweet birds, all quietly proclaim, "What a foolish wisdom it is to prefer the cold tomb to this curious and beautiful earth." The Christian who longs too keenly for heaven must also reject the living world that keeps him from heaven. Such a Christian welcomes death and, in a way, cultivates dying a little everyday.

This poem can be seen as Dickinson's renunciation of a way of life that would have one pass through this "Castle" without ever noticing or enjoying it. While she may reject death and those who desire it above life, she does not reject Resurrection or the Christian hope in an afterlife; her aim is an emphatic hymn to life. We should keep in mind when reading this version that this poem is one of the few ever to appear during her lifetime. She allowed her friend Samuel Bowles to publish it in his newspaper, *The Springfield Republican*, in the issue of March 1, 1862, under the title, "The Sleeping." If this version had been openly anti-Christian, neither she nor Bowles would have published it.

Yet the version of this poem that she sent six weeks later to her literary adviser, Thomas W. Higginson, is another matter. The second stanza of that version reads,

> Grand go the Years—in the Crescent—above them—
> Worlds scoop their Arcs—
> And Firmaments—row—
> Diadems—drop—and Doges—surrender—
> Soundless as dots—on a Disc of Snow—

These images are drawn from the cosmos rather than from the earth's natural phenomena. Instead of offering a mood of promise and familiarity, they suggest a force of relentless power and indifference. Instead of rebirth, they suggest a single-directed movement toward a goal that is not man-centered. In the face of cosmic power, human power appears insignificant. No religious consolation appears in this stanza, and it stands as an antithesis to the first stanza. Meek souls may await resurrection, but extinction is all that there is.

Time is marked in this second stanza not by hours, as it is in the first stanza, but by centuries and by the slow movement of planets and constellations in their orbits and drifts. On earth monarchies fall and leaders surrender with no affect upon the progress of the universe. In Charles R. Anderson's discussion of the poem, he offers ample evidence to suggest that "Disc of Snow" refers to the Milky

Way.[8] In the light of his observation, mankind's identity and achievements are seen by Emily as insignificant specks in the great whirling cloud of solar systems.

Where the first version of the poem offered hope in renewed and continued life, the second version envisions personal annihilation and absorption by a cold and indifferent universe. As for which version offers Dickinson's final statement on the subject, we find it impossible to say, since she permitted both versions to come to us. Taken together, they reflect the mind of the poet who could write in later life to Judge Otis Lord, "On subjects of which we know nothing . . . we both believe, and disbelieve a hundred times an Hour, which keeps Believing nimble" (*L*, III, 728).

CHAPTER 3

This Mortal Life

CLOSELY related to Emily Dickinson's religious poetry are her poems on the subject of death. In both she seeks answers to final questions about existence, purpose, and destiny; in both she boldly pursues a sense of understanding wherever the answer may lead, sometimes at the expense of peace and consolation. She was painfully aware, too, that death is the secret gateway to the other side where once and for all her doubts about religious matters would either vanish or be confirmed. An implicit aim in much of her death poetry is to risk getting close to the secret of death in the hope that she might glimpse what lies beyond. Sometimes, however, the thought of death strikes terror so deeply into her soul that she shuns the vicious trick played on unassuming mankind by a despotic God. At certain moments, death can become for Dickinson a welcome relief from pain, thought, and instability.

In almost six hundred poems she explored the nature of death as completely as any American poet ever dared. Her poems range over the physical as well as the psychological and emotional aspects of death. She looked at death from the point of view of both the living and the dying. She went so far as to imagine her own death, the loss of her own body, and the journey of her soul to the unknown. Finally, she personified death and breathed so much complexity and power of character into him that he became one of American literature's protean figures.

Her fixation on death has been attributed to a number of rational explanations. New England Calvinism and the nineteenth-century sentimental-romantic tradition were both obsessed with death in their own way, and both were part of her background and environment. Dickinson was also greatly affected by the early loss of young close friends such as Sophia Holland, Leonard Humphrey, and Benjamin Newton, all of whom died before she reached maturity; and her letters from the period reveal the melancholy states produced in her by their deaths. Millicent Todd Bingham, in *Emily Dickinson's Home*, reminds us of the lower medical and health standards of nineteenth-century America when common illnesses frequently developed into fatal ones and when many fatal diseases which are nearly unheard of today were prevalent in Dickinson's Amherst. "Furthermore," Bingham writes, "the Dickinson orchard adjoined the burying ground where the final rites took place. Every funeral procession must pass their house. The wonder is, not that Emily as a young girl thought and often wrote about death, but that any buoyancy of spirit remained."[1]

Two psychological interpretations have been advanced to explain Dickinson's unusual interest in death. Clark Griffith has suggested a Freudian interpretation: "Certainly Miss Dickinson would appear to possess, in rare abundance, each classic symptom of the death wish—not only the tendency to brood about death, but likewise the simultaneous fear-and-fascination which prompts the brooding, and in which, again and again, the brooding must always culminate."[2] And in John Cody's psychological study of Dickinson, *After Great Pain*, he enumerates the emotional sources of her preoccupation with death: "(1) fears of abandonment; (2) projection of anger; and (3) guilt feelings toward her mother."[3]

However others may describe her interest about death, we need not ignore Dickinson's own testaments about what was in her mind and heart. To Higginson she wrote, "I sing, as the Boy does by the Burying Ground—because I am afraid" (*L*, II, 404). She restated this idea in one of her poems, "I sing to use the Waiting . . . To Keep the Dark away" (*P*, 850; II, 639). Surrounded by death, by darkness, writing poetry became for her an act of courage meant to affirm her fragile life. With her great creative spirit, she transformed human frailty, fear, and anxiety into the highest levels of art; and she wrote away a measure of her terror by facing it squarely. In a moment of clear self-evaluation, she summarized her motive and achievement in the following poem:

I made my soul familiar—with her extremity—
That at the last, it should not be a novel Agony—
But she, and Death, acquainted—
Meet tranquilly, as friends—
Salute, and pass, without a Hint—
And there, the Matter ends— (*P*, 412; I, 321)

I *The Dying*

A large category of Dickinson's death poems focus on the physical aspects of dying, and we are invited to contemplate a corpse or a living body at the moment it becomes a corpse. These poems range from the reverential to the sentimental, from the eulogistic to the macabre. A few seem tasteless and amateurish; others are filled with a sympathetic understanding for the frailty of flesh. A poem such as "I like a look of Agony" (*P*, 241; I, 174), in which she descriptively enumerates the observable bodily changes that occur at the moment of death, or the poem "I've seen a Dying Eye" (*P*, 547; II, 419) with its description of the stages of death in terms of the appearance of the eyeball, seem gruesome, clinical, and lacking in the humane sensitivity that we might expect of a poet. To the other extreme, Dickinson can be the damp-eyed and sentimental poet in a group of poems such as "Some, too fragile for winter winds" (*P*, 141; I, 100); "On such a night, or such a night" (*P*, 146; I, 104–5); "She died—*this* was the way she died" (*P* 150; I, 107); " 'Twas the old—road—through pain" (*P*, 344; I, 275–76); "If anybody's friend be dead" (*P*, 509; II, 390–91); "Here, where the Daisies fit my Head" (*P*, 1037; II, 735). These poems offer the emotional complexity of only greeting-card verse and lack a mature understanding of the real nature of death. In these poems she is reminiscent of several popular nineteenth-century writers such as N. P. Willis, Donald Grant Mitchell, and Lydia Sigourney who made a career out of sentimentally combining the themes of love and death for magazines and gift-book annuals.

But we begin to see Dickinson's special achievement in the poem "She lay as if at play" in which she transforms the platitudes and conventions of funeral writing into significant poetry:

> She lay as if at play
> Her life had leaped away—
> Intending to return—
> But not so soon—
>
> Her merry Arms, half dropt—
> As if for lull of sport—
> An instant had forgot—
> The Trick to start—
>
> Her dancing Eyes—ajar—
> As if their Owner were

Still sparkling through
For fun—at you—

Her Morning at the door—
Devising, I am sure—
To force her sleep—
So light—so deep—

(*P*, 369; I, 294)

The death of a child is a pitiable occurrence which could easily lend itself in the hands of a lesser artist to maudlin commentaries on the idealization of innocence and youth, as well as to stock characterizations of the weeping mother or of the blackhearted villain, death. But Dickinson expertly adjusts the music and images of her poem to avoid the sentimental; and, to gain the reader's compassion, she focuses on the girl, her vitality and playfulness. The meter of the poem, iambic trimeter with an ending dimeter line, is quick moving and light and has a singsong quality to it. Few words in the poem are longer than two syllables; and, while not all the rhymes are perfect, a simple *aabb* pattern emerges. These musical qualities are meant to reflect and emphasize the playful and whimsical qualities of the young girl. Furthermore, in almost every line there is a word which, while it applies to the attitude of the lifeless body, also suggests the energy and activity of the girl when she was living: "play," "leaped," "merry," "sport," "instant," "trick," "start," "dancing," "sparkling," "fun," "devising," "light." The poem becomes, then, not so much a poem about death or about a dead girl as a tribute to life, to the life and personality of the young girl. Our sympathies are engaged not by playing upon our morbid curiosities but by engaging our understanding and appreciation for the beauty of this young girl when she was alive.

Emily Dickinson considered it a necessity and an honor to be present at the bedside of a loved one about to die. In "The World—feels dusty/When we stop to Die," she expresses her wish to be the one chosen to bring comfort during the final moments of life:

Mine be the Ministry
When thy Thirst comes—
Dews of Thessaly, to fetch—
And Hybla Balms—

(*P*, 715; II, 548)

In another poem she pleads with a loved one that she be notified of impending death:

> Promise This—When You be Dying—
> Some shall summon Me—
> Mine belong Your latest Sighing—
> Mine—to Belt Your Eye—

The poem develops into an elaborate fantasy of all the things she will do for the deceased. Its extravagance has a ring of artificial contrivance to it, but her feeling of privilege is clearly sincere:

> Mine—to guard Your Narrow Precinct—
> To seduce the Sun
> Longest on Your South, to linger,
> Largest Dews of Morn
>
> To demand, in Your low favor
> Lest the Jealous Grass
> Greener lean—Or fonder cluster
> Round some other face—
>
> Mine to supplicate Madonna—
> If Madonna be
> Could behold so far a Creature—
>
> (*P*, 648; II, 498–99)

Dickinson's wish to be present for these final acts of tender charity approaches a macabre insistence when in another poem in which she petitions, "If I may have it, when it's dead" (*P*, 577; II, 441–42). She is asking for the body of her dead friend, and she pictures throughout the poem an intimate conversation between herself and the beloved corpse. She ends the poem with a rare but shocking necrophilic suggestion, "Forgive me, if to stroke thy frost/ Outvisions Paradise!"

But, in another poem, witnessing death has a value for the living that is rational and more accessible to the reader. It is a lesson in courage that frees us from the fear of death and prepares us for the moment when we ourselves shall die:

> 'Tis so appalling—it exhilarates—
> So over Horror, it half Captivates—

The Soul stares after it, secure—
To know the worst, leaves no dread more—

To scan a Ghost, is faint—
But grappling, conquers it—
How easy, Torment, now—
Suspense kept sawing so—

Watching how a death happens removes both the suspense and the fear of it that existed in imagined versions of death. "Looking at Death, is Dying" she says later in the poem; and she suggests how, like watching a theatrical tragedy, we may be purged of our fear and set free to enjoy life:

It sets the Fright at liberty—
And Terror's free—
Gay, Ghastly, Holiday!

(*P*, 281; I, 200–201)

But the closing line of the poem, by juxtaposing "gay" and "ghastly," reminds us how uneasy our freedom is, since it can never completely put aside the specter of death.

Her reflections while witnessing the moment of death or during the hour or so immediately following were acutely painful ones in which the shortness and pathos of ordinary life are seen in relation to the irrevocable finality of death. In "How many times these low feet staggered" (*P*, 187; I, 135–36), Dickinson wonders how often this simple housewife struggled to endure the cares and the burdens of daily life. But she despairs of finding an answer from the woman who is now as forever beyond the reach of the living as unresponsive, immovable metal:

How many times these low feet staggered—
Only the soldered mouth can tell—
Try—can you stir the awful rivet—
Try—can you lift the hasps of steel!

Stroke the cool forehead—hot so often—
Lift—if you care—the listless hair—
Handle the adamantine fingers
Never a thimble—more—shall wear—

With the image of the thimble Dickinson invites us to a more intimate look at the woman's life. In the last stanza she pictures a room that is beginning to show the absence of the good housewife's daily attention:

> Buzz the dull flies—on the chamber window—
> Brave—shines the sun through the freckled pane—
> Fearless—the cobweb swings from the ceiling—
> Indolent Housewife—in Daisies—lain!

The thimble, the flies, the pane freckled with dirt, and the cobweb are samples from the household with which this woman had busied herself to death. With fine irony in the last line, Dickinson makes the point that only in death may a housewife find rest from the ceaseless toil of her station.

In two other poems of the same order, the poet reflects upon the awesome changes that occur in death and that render strange and unrecognizable what had been so precious and familiar. In "This that would greet—an hour ago," Dickinson is struck by the sudden immeasurable distance that separates her from a deceased friend. Only a short time before, she reflects, they would have greeted each other warmly; but the coldness and immobility of death now divide them. Now nothing, she muses, not even "a Guest from Paradise," can make this body warm or move. Perplexed, she addresses the reader: "Match me the Silver Reticence—/Match me the Solid Calm—" (*P*, 778; II, 588). In "These—saw Visions" (*P*, 758; II, 577), she tries to remove the contortions of death and to restore to normal expression the face and the body of a woman who has suddenly died. The eyes, cheeks, mouth, hair, hands, and feet of the deceased are tenderly adjusted and positioned as they were best remembered in life.

With the poem, "A Clock stopped" (*P*, 287; I, 206), Dickinson is concerned with the precise moment—the instant of death—and with the final, irreversible stroke of living time. She transforms a commonplace object, a mantel clock, into a metaphysical conceit for depicting the end of life. Using fable, cliché, and the superstitious belief that the clock stops when its owner dies, Dickinson compares death to the irreparable breakdown of a finely made Swiss clock. The first stanza opens with a halved first line that emphasizes the sudden cessation of life and time:

A Clock stopped—
Not the Mantel's—
Geneva's farthest skill
Can't put the puppet bowing—
That just now dangled still—

An awe came on the Trinket!
The Figures hunched, with pain—
Then quivered out of Decimals—
Into Degreeless Noon—

Not the best watchmaker in Geneva, a world center for fine timepieces, can revive the heart of this stopped clock. Just as men are suddenly struck dead during their daily routines, these figures that dance out of the clock at the stroke of the hour are stilled and bent in the middle of their performance. Bitterly she suggests that perhaps we are like the trinkets in the clock. Like the puppets who bow in a parody of courtesy and who do over and over again their proud little routines, we were made to do so by some great puppet maker, until death freezes us and exposes the absurdity of our behavior. She pictures eternity as noon, as she has in several other poems.[4] At noon the sun overhead appears to stand still, and the hands of the clock have run a complete circle of three hundred and sixty degrees and are superimposed over one another so no angle or degrees separate them. In a sense, noon is zero hour, the start, or as in death, the end of a cycle.

The next two stanzas shift our attention from the dead to the futile efforts of the living to restore a life forever closed:

It will not stir for Doctor's—
This Pendulum of snow—
The Shopman importunes it—
While cool—concernless No—

Nods from the Gilded pointers—
Nods from the Seconds slim—
Decades of Arrogance between
The Dial life—
And Him—

"No," the indifferent negative of the third stanza echoed in the "Nods" of the fourth stanza, is the emphatic denial offered to the doctor and the shopman who try to restore life. The pendulum, or force and movement of life, are referred to as "of snow," a favorite symbol of Dickinson's for the cold, blank condition of death. The soul of the deceased is already far out of the reach of human time; it is separated from "the Dial life" by the prospect of "Decades of Arrogance," the overbearing burden of eternity.

Perhaps Dickinson's greatest description of the moment of death is to be found in "I heard a Fly buzz—when I died" (*P*, 465; I, 358), a poem universally considered one of her masterpieces. Through an imaginative retrospect of her own death, Dickinson renders with convincing and insightful detail the last sensations of a dying person. The "Fly," discussed and debated as much as any symbol in American literature, remains an appropriately complex and suggestive presence:

> I heard a Fly buzz—when I died—
> The Stillness in the Room
> Was like the Stillness in the Air—
> Between the Heaves of Storm—
>
> The Eyes around—had wrung them dry—
> And Breaths were gathering firm
> For that last Onset—when the King
> Be witnessed—in the Room—

The somber and hushed atmosphere of the opening lines are jarred by the ludicrous presence of a buzzing fly. All in the room is silent and still, yet filled with the anxious expectation of those caught in the eye of a storm. It was hoped among traditional Christians of Dickinson's age that the last words or gestures of the dying person would indicate the destiny of the soul. So the sorrowing observers of the second stanza stand in breathless anticipation of that final moment when Death will appear to escort the deceased with all pomp and ceremony to her heavenly reward.

But Dickinson, with skeptical irony, brings the poem to a close without the expected vision of immortality:

> I willed my Keepsakes—Signed away
> What portion of me be
> Assignable—and then it was
> There interposed a Fly—

With Blue—uncertain stumbling Buzz—
Between the light—and me—
And then the Windows failed—and then
I could not see to see—

Her final minutes are spent signing away her collectables and contemplating a fly. That great moment when she might have expected confirmation of glory, or when those near her might have hoped for a glimpse of the beyond, is lost in triviality and petty annoyance.

A note of despair is also present. The fly separates the dying person from the light—not just the light from the windows, but the radiant light of Paradise as well. The fly, a blowfly as Caroline Hogue has noted, is a grim omen of the decay that awaits the body in the grave.[5] In closing the poem by fixing this image in the mind, Dickinson gives up the hope of immortality by ruefully suggesting that only the maggot will have the ultimate dominion of the human heart.

II *The Living*

In other poems, Dickinson shifted her attention from the dying to the living; and she focused on those left behind who had to cope with sorrow and learn to readjust their lives. In "There's been a Death, in the Opposite House" (*P*, 389; I, 306–7), Dickinson observes how humans try to divert their suffering and loss through ritual and ceremony. Looking from her window at the house across the road, she knows "by the numb look/Such Houses have" that someone has died. The sudden increase in activity in the house is the formal and mechanical kind that death imposes on the distressed living:

The Neighbors rustle in and out—
The Doctor—drives away—
A Window opens like a Pod—
Abrupt—mechanically—

Somebody flings a Mattress out—
The Children hurry by—

Other solemn figures arrive and behave with typically ceremonious detachment: the minister who "goes stiffly in," the milliner, and "the Man/Of the Appalling Trade." After witnessing the regularized, hushed behavior surrounding the house, the narrator observes:

> There'll be that Dark Parade—
>
> Of Tassels—and of Coaches—soon—
> It's easy as a Sign—
> The Intuition of the News—
> In just a Country Town—

In another poem the instinctive formality of the living, when confronted with death, approaches a condition of nearly total emotional suppression. The verbal style of "The last Night that She lived" (*P*, 1100; II, 773–74), as Clark Griffith has thoroughly documented, "creates an atmosphere of rigidly curbed hysteria."[6] The language is plain, the syntax is occasionally twisted, and the rhymes are unmusical. In addition, the uniformly toneless description of the entire event contributes to the strained objectivity and benumbed coolness Dickinson is striving to maintain. The poem opens by indicating how the presence of death makes the ordinary appear extraordinary; the unseen, glaring:

> The last Night that She lived
> It was a Common Night
> Except the Dying—this to Us
> Made Nature different
>
> We noticed smallest things—
> Things overlooked before
> By this great light upon our Minds
> Italicized—as 'twere.

The observers can do little but pass in and out of the sick room and feel "a Blame/That Others could exist/While She must finish quite." They wait in silence while she passes away, "Too jostled were Our Souls to speak." When the moment of death passes, the mourners routinely adjust the deceased and are left with an overwhelming emptiness as they try to understand the meaning of what has happened:

And We—We placed the Hair—
And drew the Head erect—
And then an awful leisure was
Belief to regulate—

Speaking of this last stanza, Brita Lindberg-Seyersted has justly observed that "The repetition of 'We' suggests the mechanical movements of the mourners and perhaps also the faltering voice of one describing the last night that the beloved woman lived."[7] The mourners are left to face their own crisis—a crisis of faith—and to try to regulate their belief to accept the death of a dearly loved.

III *Personifications of Death*

Throughout a lifetime of observation and reflection, death had become for Emily Dickinson a familiar reality that was capable of imaginative embodiment in characteristic guises. Despite her description of death in an early poem,

Dust is the only Secret—
Death, the only One
You cannot find out all about
In his "native town"

(*P*, 153; I, 109–10)

some of her most enduring poems are those which have made this unknowable, frightening force into a character capable of being understood in terms of common experience.

Among appropriate personifications, Death appears as a democrat in a number of poems, the great equalizer, the force which claims without discrimination men and women from every station in life:

Color—Caste—Denomination—
These—are Time's Affair—
Death's diviner Classifying
Does not know they are—

(*P*, 970; II 702)

In this poem Death puts aside all differences which separate the living and his "large—Democratic fingers/Rub away the Brand." White, blond, or black are all the same to him; and "His Obscuring" makes standards of difference among the living seem implausible.

Again, the image of the democrat controls this poem: "Not any higher stands the Grave/For Heroes than for Men" (*P*, 1256; III, 871). All people, the young as well as the very old, "The Beggar and his Queen" must appease this democrat.

To the other extreme, the solemnity and the formality that surround Death suggest his associations with royalty. In "One dignity delays for all" (*P*, 98; I, 76), he assures for everyone "One mitred Afternoon" when they shall be part of his magnificent procession with coach, footmen, and dignified entourage. Bells will ring during the march, and there will be a solemn service with a hundred raised hats. But he is a democratic despot who exalts the most humble:

> How pomp surpassing ermine
> When simple You, and I,
> Present our meek escutcheon
> And claim the rank to die!

Similarly, in "Wait till the Majesty of Death/Invests so mean a brow" (*P*, 171; I, 125–26), Death bestows all the highest honors of royalty upon the lowliest:

> Around this quiet Courtier
> Obsequious Angels wait!
> Full royal is his Retinue!
> Full purple is his state!
>
> A Lord, might dare to lift the Hat
> To such a Modest Clay
> Since that My Lord, "the Lord of Lords"
> Receives unblushingly!

In another group of poems the frightful persistence of Death is not cast with a human analogy. "It's coming—the postponeless Creature" (*P*, 390; I, 307–8) preserves the horror surrounding death by denying it recognizable human characteristics. Death is referred to as a "Creature," and the pronoun "it" is used throughout the poem to emphasize the separation between Death and the world of the living. A more fully drawn picture of Death as a creature utterly without recognizable human form is to be found in one of her rare ballads, "The Frost of Death was on the Pane" (*P*, 1136; II, 797). In this poem, the friends of the female victim try to hold back Death and to place themselves between her and Death; but their attempt is futile for "easy as the narrow Snake/He forked his way along." Their helplessness enrages them, and they pursue Death as they would a beast or monster to his hiding place:

> And then our wrath begun—
> We hunted him to his Ravine
> We chased him to his Den—

They are bewildered by his power and frustrated at being his victims. The poem closes with an expression of cosmic sorrow that we exist in a universe that does not offer an explanation to or a consolation for man:

> We hated Death and hated Life
> And nowhere was to go—
> Than Sea and continent there is
> A larger—it is Woe.

Without a doubt Emily Dickinson's richest personifications of Death are those which portray him as a gentleman caller or as a suitor. "Because I could not stop for Death" and "Death is the supple Suitor" are two of her more popular poems which have as their controlling image a well-realized rendition of the complex character of Death and which are also remarkably succinct statements of Dickinson's own ambivalent reactions to death. The first poem, "Because I could not stop for Death" (*P*, 712; II 546), is a dramatic representation of the passage from this world of the living to the afterlife. The event is couched in a metaphorical use of an activity familiar enough to men and women of the nineteenth century—a formal but friendly drive in a carriage in the country of a gentleman and his intended lady. The gentleman in question, however, is Death himself; and the lady is an imagined persona of the poet. She is looking back upon how life had been before he came, and her memories are infused with the subtle tensions of one not completely at rest. The opening of the poem has an understated casualness of tone:

> Because I could not stop for Death—
> He kindly stopped for me—
> The Carriage held but just Ourselves—
> And Immortality.

We slowly drove—He knew no haste
And I had put away
My labor and my leisure too,
For His Civility—

In the first line the persona is too busy and too contented as she lives her life to bother to stop for the gentleman's call; but, through his kindness and consideration, she is compelled at last to go with him. In the third line, the dramatic scene is set in the carriage. The situation is one of intimacy—"the Carriage held but just Ourselves." He has called on her as a beau; and, like a true gentleman, he has included a chaperone, "Immortality."

The first line of the second stanza indicates the peacefulness and pleasantness surrounding an appointment with a beau. He drives leisurely, without haste—ironically, as if they had all the time in the world. She who could not stop for Death in the first stanza is completely captivated by him in the second and third lines of this stanza. He is such an artful charmer that she needs neither labor nor leisure, for in his "Civility" he has taken care of everything. By the third stanza, they are nearing the edge of town:

We passed the School, where Children strove
At Recess—in the Ring—
We passed the Fields of Gazing Grain—
We passed the Setting Sun—

Or rather—He passed Us—
The Dews drew quivering and chill—
For only Gossamer, my Gown—
My Tippet—only Tulle—

The seemingly disparate elements of children, "Gazing Grain," and "Setting Sun" achieve a homogeneity through the perceptions of the maiden. As Eunice Glenn has noted, "They are all perceived as elements in an experience from which the onlooker has withdrawn."[8] The sensations that the dying lady experiences, are transferred, therefore, to these parts of the world. She is gazing, and the notion is transferred to the grain; she is "setting," and this notion is transferred to the sun. The children "striving" at recess is a subtle preparation for the stasis described in the succeeding images. In addition, the three elements summarize the progress and passage of a lifetime. As Charles R. Anderson described them, "The seemingly disparate parts of this are fused into a vivid reenactment of the mortal experience. It includes the three stages of youth, maturity, and age, the cycle of day from morning to evening, and even a suggestion of seasonal progression from the year's upspring through ripening to decline."[9]

In the fourth stanza, the lady is getting closer to death; for "The Dews" now grow "quivering and chill" upon her skin, the traditional associations of the coldness of death. This calls to mind another of Dickinson's poems in which Death is depicted as the frost, that "blonde Assassin" (*P*, 1624; III, 1114). In the third line, however, the lady is still holding onto life by offering a rational explanation about her chill. She is not really dying, she seems to say; she is cold simply because her gown is thin. But she cannot escape her death, for she reveals even in her garments the dying influence: her gown is gossamer, a substance associated with spirits and otherworldliness; and her tippet, made of lace, is something one might expect to see around the shoulders of a deceased woman lying in repose.

In the fifth stanza, they have arrived at a country cemetery:

We paused before a House that seemed
A Swelling of the Ground—
The Roof was scarcely visible—
The Cornice—in the Ground—

Since then—'tis Centuries—and yet
Feels shorter than the Day
I first surmised the Horses Heads
Were toward Eternity—

The House is the house of death, a fresh grave, sketched only with a few details. The roof is a small tombstone; and the cornice, the molding around a coffin's lid, is already placed "in the Ground." The lady is alone now; her gentleman friend has vanished unexplained.

In the sixth stanza the words "first surmised" contributes a note of ironic surprise. All along, then, she did not realize where her kind, intimate, slow-driving, civil suitor was taking her. It was not until after the school children, the "Gazing Grain," the "Setting Sun," and the "Swelling of the Ground" that she began to realize where she was heading. She had, therefore, apparently been tricked, seduced, and then abandoned. In these terms, then, Dickinson is being terribly ironic throughout the poem. She is saying "kindly," "slowly drove," and "Civility" in retrospect through clenched teeth. The mood of intimacy created in the carriage is ironically suffocating. The characteristic peacefulness of the drive, then, is really *rigor mortis*. Also, the intimations of mortality scattered throughout the poem are dramatic ironies of the most subtle and provocative sort, since the reader himself is not fully aware of their import until the very end of the poem.

In its depiction of Death on one hand as the courtly suitor and on the other as the fraudulent seducer, the poem reflects a basic ambiguity toward death and immortality characteristic of Emily Dickinson. Is death a release from a lifetime of work and suffering, is it the gateway to a lasting peace in paradise, or is it simply a cold, mindless annihilation?

If she held both versions in abeyance throughout her lifetime, her emphasis in the next poem is clearly upon annihilation:

Death is the supple Suitor
That wins at last—
It is a stealthy Wooing
Conducted first
By pallid innuendoes
And dim approach
But brave at last with Bugles
And a bisected Coach
It bears away in triumph
To Troth unknown
And Kindred as responsive
As Porcelain.

(*P*, 1445; III, 1001–2)

The "supple Suitor" of the first line in the poem is even more sinister than the "kindly," civil beau of the last poem. This suitor is absolutely adaptable and will assume any guise, use any methods to win his lady, as the second line suggests—"wins at last." His wooing is "stealthy," his suggestions "pallid," and his approach "dim." He is the deathly parallel of the attentive lover. The forms of his courtship are acceptable and traditional, but they are covered with suggestions of death.

After he has won her, he comes to carry her off to her wedding, "brave at last with Bugles/And a bisected Coach." The royal marriage, however, bears the maiden away "To Troth unknown/And

Kindred as responsive/As Porcelain." In these last few lines, we are given a terrifying view of the grave. Her destiny may be "unknown," but we can be sure it is not heaven. Under no circumstances is heaven associated with inhabitants who are as *un*responsive as cold, hard, white porcelain. This marriage is to Death, not to Christ; and the wedding bower is the family grave, not heaven. Eternity in this poem has a strong suggestion of being a mindless isolation—a condition of oblivion. She will be placed among kindred whose responses are like porcelain, and porcelain figures are like corpses with cold, silent, insensate stares.

CHAPTER 4

Versions of Love

I *Lord, Wadsworth, and Bowles*

AS we suggested earlier in Chapter 1, much interest has been shown in identifying the men Emily Dickinson loved. Much of this interest has resulted in absurd speculation, but the facts—both the simple and the complex—point to her genuine love of one man late in her life and to an impassioned, unrequited love for another during her young womanhood. The man she loved was Otis P. Lord, who had been a close friend of Edward Dickinson and a frequent visitor to the house, an eminent lawyer, and member of the state supreme court from 1875 to 1882. When her father died in 1874, Emily turned instinctively to Lord as an old family friend for consolation. After Lord's wife died in 1877, bringing to an end a happy marriage of nearly thirty-five years, he and Emily were drawn closer together. By the summer of 1878, although nineteen years separated them—he was sixty-six and she was forty-seven—they realized that their friendship had developed into a mature and mutual love. Marriage was very likely contemplated, but Emily persisted in her poetry and her isolation.

Her letters to Lord survive in only partial drafts, but they reveal a peaceful and happy heart rejoicing at last in the warmth and security of a sincere love. One of her letters to him shows a frank expression of her fervent heart:

> My lovely Salem smiles at me. I seek his Face so often—but I have done with guises.
>
> I confess that I love him—I rejoice that I love him—I thank the maker of Heaven and Earth—that gave him me to love—the exultation floods me. I cannot find my Channel—the Creek turns Sea—at thought of thee—
>
> Will you punish me? "Involuntary Bankruptcy," how could that be Crime?

Incarcerate me in yourself—rosy penalty threading with you this lovely maze, which is not Life or Death—though it has the intangibleness of one, and the flush of the other—waking for your sake on Day made magical with you before I went. (*L*, II, 614–15)

As much in love as she was, however, she chose not to abandon her mode of life for marriage. That she completely understood what she was refusing is demonstrated in a letter filled with the language of intimacy desired though denied:

It is strange that I miss you at night so much when I was never with you—but the punctual love invokes you soon as my eyes are shut—and I wake warm with the want sleep had almost filled—I dreamed last week that you had died—and one had carved a statue of you and I was asked to unveil it—and I said what I had not done in Life I would not in death when your loved eyes could not forgive—. . . .
Lest I had been too frank was often my fear—How could I long to give who never saw your natures Face— (*L*, III, 663–64)

Though they never married she did wear a ring he gave her for the rest of her life; and, a few weeks after his death in 1884, she suffered a nervous collapse which marked the beginning of a protracted illness from which she died less than two years later. As a final testament of their love, when Emily died, Lavinia put two heliotropes in the coffin by her sister's hand, as she said, 'to take to Judge Lord.'

That Emily Dickinson loved another man earlier in her life, during the late 1850s through the early 1860s, seems likely; and it is also most likely that this man was already married, had a family, and was unaware that he was the object of her love. Her love, therefore, was secret and unrequited. The most probable candidates that have been named are the Reverend Charles Wadsworth and Mr. Samuel Bowles. The conjectured first meeting between Dickinson and Wadsworth probably took place in March, 1855, on her trip home after visiting her father, then a congressman in Washington. Dickinson stayed two weeks in Philadelphia, and it is believed she met him there where he was serving as pastor of the Arch Street Presbyterian Church.

Although not an original theologian, he was considered a powerful and dramatic preacher with solidly orthodox beliefs and sincere moral intensity. We are sure of only two visits by him to Amherst, one in March, 1860, and another in August, 1880. There are no letters extant from her to him, and the only letter from him, undated and unsigned, is clearly not of a romantic nature. The letter simply offers her his prayers and spiritual consolation for an unnamed affliction that she had apparently written to him about. After his death in 1882, Dickinson began a correspondence with Wadsworth's friends, the brothers Charles and James Clark. What emerges from this correspondence is how very little Dickinson knew about Wadsworth's personal life, for she actually had to ask if he had a brother or sister. The Clark brothers sent her two volumes of Wadsworth's sermons and his picture, and they exchanged some personal reminiscences of the man with her.

Another possible candidate, the one recently accepted as the likeliest, is Samuel Bowles. He was the dynamic editor of the *Springfield Republican* who transformed that newspaper from an ordinary town weekly into one of the most influential dailies in America. He and his wife became regular visitors and correspondents with the Dickinsons around 1858. His was a passionate personality; and, ambitious and widely traveled, he easily made warm friends among men and women alike. Dickinson's extensive correspondence with him lasted until his death in 1878, and her letters to him are warm and friendly, playful yet never overtly passionate. She occasionally sent him her poetry; and, of the few poems published in her lifetime, five appeared in the pages of the *Springfield Republican*—the valentine, "'Sic transit gloria mundi,'" "I taste a liquor never brewed," "Safe in their alabaster chambers," "Blazing in gold and quenching in purple," and "A narrow fellow in the grass."[1]

Clearly, both Wadsworth and Bowles cared for Dickinson in some way; both were respectable and responsible men of the world and were appealing in their own way. An attraction for either man would have been perfectly natural, although acting upon that attraction would have violated every code known to her. Because no evidence at all suggests that either man ever responded to her in an overtly passionate way, or that either man even knew of her feelings, it is believed that whatever attraction she felt flourished in the secrecy of her own heart. This need for secrecy, as well as the resulting frustration and tension it produced, is believed to account in part, at least, for the anguish she suffered during the critical years 1858 to 1864, and to be contributing factors to her development as a poet.

II *The "Master" Letters*

One of the strangest pieces of evidence from the period that suggests Dickinson's secret and tormenting love are the three drafts of letters found among her papers addressed to an unnamed "Master." They are puzzling documents not only because of their cryptic content but also because of their distorted rhetoric that is apparently the product of her severe tension. They are painfully moving letters to read because the voice in them pleads desperately for love and attention, and complains pitiably of being denied. The sense of rejection and unfulfilled desire echoes throughout their lines:

> I am older—tonight, Master—but the love is the same—so are the moon and the crescent. If it had been God's will that I might breathe where you breathed—and find the place—myself—at night—if I [can] never forget that I am not with you—and that sorrow and frost are nearer than I—if I wish with a might I cannot repress—that mine were the Queen's place—. . . .
>
> I don't know what you can do for it—thank you—Master—but if I had the Beard on my cheek—like you—and you—had Daisy's petals—and you cared so for me—what would become of you? Could you forget me in fight, or flight—or the foreign land? Could'nt Carlo, and you and I walk in the meadows an hour—and nobody care but the Bobolink—and *his*—a *silver* scruple? I used to think when I died—I could see you—so I died as fast as I could—but the "Corporation" are going Heaven too so [Eternity] wont be sequestered—now [at all]—. . . .
>
> I want to see you more—Sir—than all I wish for in this world—and the wish—altered a little—will be my only one—for the skies. (*L*, II, 374–75)

A large part of our difficulty with these letters stems from the fact that we cannot identify the "Master" they are addressed to; therefore, many of the references and terms remain obscured and debatable. Ruth Miller's analysis of the "Master" letters appears to be the most thorough and convincing.[2] She believes they were never sent, but were written for Dickinson's own eyes as relief for her feelings of frustration at the indifference of Samuel Bowles. Miller's close examination of the letters reveals that they served as the source material for later poems and letters that Dickinson did send to Bowles. Miller's evidence for the similarities is based "on the correspondence of imagery, on paraphrase of subject matter, on similarity of allusions, on identical questions, and on the likeness of emotional tone." Placing the "Master" letters alongside poems and letters to Bowles, she finds "the same exaggerated modesty, the almost painful self-deprecation; . . . the same appeals, the barbs, the complaints, the cryptic ironies."[3] Her analysis, both of the content and of the language in the letters, strongly suggests that the "Master" and the early lover were Samuel Bowles.

The facts and forces in any person's emotional life are complex and usually sufficiently private to make reconstruction difficult, if not altogether impossible. In the case of Emily Dickinson, an elusive personality who clung to her privacy perhaps more than anyone else in literary history, the hidden areas of her life may prove to be forever impervious to full illumination. Whether the man she loved in her early years was indeed Bowles, or Wadsworth, or some other person yet to be revealed, the fact remains that during the period from 1858 to 1864 she not only learned about the beauty and the pain of human love but transformed her experience into some of the finest lyrics in the English language.

III *The Bee and the Worm*

The first grouping of love poems to be examined focuses on the physical aspects of desire. In a largely allegorical mode, Dickinson considered the influence of the male upon the female, emphasized the power of physical attraction, and expressed a mixture of fear and fascination for the mysterious magnetism between the sexes. Her lighter treatments of these themes appear in the poems which describe a lover-bee who symbolically assaults a flower. In "A Bee his burnished Carriage," the poet depicts the bee as boldly taking his pleasure of the rose and of then leaving her humbled by the rapture he has caused her to feel:

A Bee his burnished Carriage
Drove boldly to a Rose—
Combinedly alighting—
Himself—his Carriage was—
The Rose received his visit
With frank tranquillity
Withholding not a Crescent
To his Cupidity—
Their Moment consummated—
Remained for him—to flee—
Remained for her—of rapture
But the humility.

(*P*, 1339; III, 925)

The bee's interest in the rose is exclusively sexual, as is hers in him. He boldly arrives and enters, and she frankly witholds "not a Crescent" of herself. The words "Cupidity," "consummated," and "rapture" lend specificity to the action suggested in the poem. The situation portrayed emphasizes the male's power, his active role as initiator of their union and pleasure, while the stationary female remains the passive recipient of his will.

However, in another poem about the lover-bee, the poet questions the status of the female when she submits and the honor of the male when he achieves his objective:

Did the Harebell loose her girdle
To the lover Bee
Would the Bee the Harebell *hallow*
Much as formerly?

Did the "Paradise"—persuaded—
Yield her moat of pearl—
Would the Eden *be* an Eden,
Or the Earl—an *Earl?*

(*P*, 213; I, 149)

The poem functions on two levels at once. The first, level questions the artificial behavior of lovers. Dickinson perceived that the roles lovers played to win each other's affection often resulted in a degradation of the person and in the loss of what was most desired. The poem asks, therefore, if the lady, who has been persuaded to yield, will be as honored as before? And will he remain the gentleman he so thoroughly portrayed himself to be? The second level concerns the larger issue relative to the possession of any object of value that is longed for. In this case the poem is attentive to the human tendency and malady of devaluing whatever is within reach, including love, and to cherish and desire whatever cannot be had. After anything is possessed, the poem asks, is not its value somewhat lessened in the owner's eyes?

One of the strangest poems in the whole Dickinson canon is the symbolically erotic "In Winter in my Room" (*P*, 1670; III, 1137–38). It is at once a graphic description of the power of sexual attraction and an analysis of the fear and repulsion it may arouse. Its imagery has invited Freudian interpretations, and its allegorical form has given the poem its status as a classic example of repressed desire.[4]

The poem opens in winter, at a time of emotional barrenness and isolation; and the lady finds in her room a harmless worm. As a precaution, she seeks to contain it with string:

In Winter in my Room
I came upon a Worm
Pink lank and warm
But as he was a worm
And worms presume
Not quite with him at home
Secured him by a string
To something neighboring
And went along.

But the worm will not remain contained; and, when she returns, she is met by a powerful snake:

A Trifle afterward
A thing occurred
I'd not believe it if I heard
But state with creeping blood
A snake with mottles rare
Surveyed my chamber floor
In feature as the worm before
But ringed with power.

The phallic imagery suggested in the first stanza is confirmed in this section. The male force explodes despite her naive attempts to restrain it, and it threatens to dominate her as it is "ringed with power." She shrinks in fear and attempts to appease it: " 'How fair you are'!/Propitiation's claw—." A dialogue ensues in which the snake toys with her just prior to his advance:

Then to a Rhythm *Slim*
Secreted in his Form
As Patterns swim
Projected him.

His rising sexual desire parallels the coiling rhythm of a snake about to attack. Fascinated, and at the same time terrified, she wavers momentarily before her sudden retreat to "a distant Town/Towns on from mine." The poem closes abruptly with what first appears to be a misplaced assertion: "This was a dream." But the line reflects the poet's determination, perhaps unconsciously, to reject the drives and feelings she has uncovered in herself.

In terms of its allegorical framework, the poem depicts a woman who is trying to rise out of a period of emotional stagnation but is confronting a situation, offered as a solution, which she is not equipped to handle. She finds a male companion that she thinks she may enjoy without fear, but she discovers that her attentions have aroused his ardor and that he threatens to break out of the controls she had established for them. His advances please and attract her; but, when she cannot shake her own deep-seated fears of masculine aggression, she retreats. In an effort to wipe her memory clean of the experience, to repress the inadequacy she felt as desire was overcome by terror, she maintains, "This was a dream."

IV *"With just the Door ajar"*

The largest category of her love poems treats of the suffering and frustration love can cause. These poems clearly have their roots in her own unhappy experience, and they are intimately related to her deepest and most private feelings. Although a number of them lack artistic control, and that sense of the universal in feeling necessary to raise them above the biographical or the personal, many of them are striking and original expressions depicting the longing for shared moments, the pain of separation, and the futility of finding happiness.

In an exuberantly imaginative poem, "What would I give to see his face?" (*P*, 247; I, 177–78), the poet professes in fantastic hyperboles what she is willing to pay in exchange for the sight of her lover. The urgency of her desire is appropriately reflected in the vigorous verbal irregularities of the poem:

> What would I give to see his face?
> I'd give—I'd give my life—of course—
> But *that* is not enough!
> Stop just a minute—let me think!
> I'd give my biggest Bobolink!
> That makes *two*—*Him*—and *Life!*
> You know who "*June*" is—
> I'd give *her*—
> Roses a day from Zanzibar—
> And Lily tubes—like Wells—

Bees—by the furlong—
Straits of Blue
Navies of Butterflies—sailed thro'—
And dappled Cowslip Dells—

Her hesitations in the second and fourth lines contribute to the sense of immediacy in the poem, and they heighten the feeling that the speaker is indeed willing to give anything right now to have her wish fulfilled. In the next stanza, she shifts to the language of business and offers " 'shares' in Primrose 'Banks'—/Daffodil Dowries—spicy 'Stocks'—. . ./Bags of Doubloons." By the close of the poem, she vows this vast accumulation of goods to any Shylock who can pledge in return "*One hour*—of her Sovereign's face!"

A more tightly structured poem that expresses the same longing to be united with the loved one is "If you were coming in the Fall" (*P*, 511; II, 392–93). In each of the first four stanzas, the poet considers larger periods of time and argues that her feeling of emptiness would be supportable if reunion could be achieved after any one of them:

If you were coming in the Fall,
I'd brush the Summer by
With half a smile, and half a spurn,
As Housewives do, a Fly.

If I could see you in a year,
I'd wind the months in balls—
And put them each in separate Drawers,
For fear the numbers fuse—

If only Centuries, delayed,
I'd count them on my Hand,
Subtracting, till my fingers dropped
Into Van Dieman's Land.

If certain, when this life was out—
That yours and mine, should be—
I'd toss it yonder, like a Rind,
And take Eternity—

But, in the last stanza, her doubt of their ever being together goads the poet to a feeling of despair:

But, now, uncertain of the length
Of this, that is between,
It goads me, like the Goblin Bee—
That will not state—its sting.

In opposition to the previous poem, which was artfully spontaneous because its form was accumulative rather than developmental, this poem is formally organized and strictly regularized. Each stanza alternates a line of iambic tetrameter with a line of iambic trimeter and closely follows the rhyme scheme *abcb*. The first four stanzas are a unit, and this unity is emphasized through the grammatical structure. Each begins with the conditional "If" and states an appropriate resolution beginning with the contracted form of "I would." Each stanza is also related to every other by containing an image drawn from the domestic scene. Finally, the entire poem is rounded off as a self-contained unit by countering the harmless fly in the first stanza with the "Goblin Bee" in the last. Taken together, then, as a pair, "What would I give to see his face?" and "If you were coming in the Fall" delineate the extremes of attitude and form that Dickinson employed in this category of poetry—from the extravagantly romantic to the formally metaphysical.

When the long-desired meeting between the lovers finally does occur, it is regrettably all too fleeting, as recorded in "There came a Day at Summer's full" (*P*, 322; I, 249–50). The emphasis in the poem is on the transcience of love, on the impermanence of human relationships, and on the anguish of knowing that all of life's joys are circumscribed by speeding time. The pleasant nature imagery of the opening stanzas gives way to religious imagery as the poem progresses, thereby suggesting the human need to replace temporal joys with promises of everlasting eternity. As time speeds by and as the meeting draws near to an end, having lasted one brief day, the lovers betroth themselves to seek eternal bliss in Christian resurrection:

The Hours slid fast—as Hours will,
Clutched tight, by greedy hands—
So faces on two Decks, look back,
Bound to opposing lands—

And so when all the time had leaked,
Without external sound

Each bound the Other's Crucifix—
We gave no other Bond—

Sufficient troth, that we shall rise—
Deposed—at length, the Grave—
To that new Marriage,
Justified—through Calvaries of Love—

As thinly hopeful as the tone of this poem is, its conclusion does look forward, nevertheless, to a life together after death despite the years of separation and suffering that must precede. In the next poem, however, despair is all there is in this life as in the next for a love impossibly ideal, impossibly demanding.

In her longest poem "I cannot live with You" *(P,* 640; II, 492–93), the poet considers in turn life, death, resurrection, and judgment; and she concludes that in every condition their love cannot be allowed to flourish. In the first two stanzas, she eliminates the possibility of a life together:

I cannot live with You—
It would be Life—
And Life is over there—
Behind the Shelf

The Sexton keeps the Key to—
Putting up
Our Life—His Porcelain—
Like a Cup—

The image of the sexton's locking up the porcelain is an apt one for depicting life; for Dickinson perceived it as it was being lived in Puritan Amherst—entirely controlled by law, custom, and duty, especially as they were established by the church and enforced on every level of society. Their love, because of its nature and magnitude, must be stifled in such an atmosphere of regulation and inhibition.

Nor can they be allowed to die together is her statement in the fourth stanza, "For One must wait/To shut the Other's Gaze down—." As unthinkable as it is to be left in this world without the other, the poet writes, still one must remain to perform the last offices for the other. In the sixth stanza, she considers the resurrection after death:

Nor could I rise—with You—
Because Your Face
Would put out Jesus'—
That New Grace.

Unlike the previous poem, "There came a day at summer's full," that anticipated a shared eternity for the lovers, this poem denies the possibility; for her idolatrous love would prevent her from acknowledging her true savior. If, on the other hand, the Lord's judgment separated them in the afterlife, she writes that she would be condemned to an eternity of desolation no matter where she was placed:

And were You lost, I would be—
Though My Name
Rang loudest
On the Heavenly fame—

And were you—saved—
And I—condemned to be
Where You were not—
That self—were Hell to Me—

Therefore, nothing remains for them but to deny themselves and to carry on separately with their lives. The poem comes to a somber conclusion with a stunning image of self-inflicted isolation as they accept their hopeless fate:

So We must meet apart—
You there—I—here—
With just the Door ajar
That Oceans are—and Prayer—
And that White Sustenance—
Despair—

A final poem in this grouping reconsiders the enforced separation, makes an attempt for comfort in prayer, but concludes with a shocking piece of heresy. "I got so I could take his name" (*P*, 293; I, 211–12), a poem of consummate artistry, renders in the first three stanzas the soul's agony because of separation through the vivid imagery of physical pain:

I got so I could take his name—
Without—Tremendous gain—
That Stop-sensation—on my Soul—
And Thunder—in the Room—

I got so I could walk across
That Angle in the floor
Where he turned so, and I turned—how—
And all our Sinews tore—

I got so I could stir the Box—
In which his letters grew
Without that forcing, in my breath—
As Staples—driven through—

The stanzas describe the painful attempt to bring under control her emotional reactions that are stimulated by the memories of her absent lover (his name, where he walked, his letters). The idiomatic phrase "I got so I could . . ." is an appropriately qualified and tentative expression for indicating that her condition is not altogether stable, that she has not quite gotten used to his absence. The pain of loss is still fresh to her senses.

In the fourth and fifth stanzas, the speaker turns to other parts of her memory for comfort. She recollects God and the unfamiliar gestures of praying:

Could dimly recollect a Grace—
I think, they call it "God"—
Renowned to ease Extremity—
When Formula, had failed—

And shape my Hands—
Petition's way,
Tho' ignorant of a word
That Ordination—utters—

Struggling to bring her emotional disturbance under control, the poet rejects the notion of pleading to the Divinity in the final stanza; for she believes He is only remotely interested in her and would consider her misery of trivial importance—as not worth his interrupting:

My Business, with the Cloud,
If any Power behind it, be,
Not subject to Despair—
It care, in some remoter way,
For so minute affair
As Misery—
Itself, too great, for interrupting—more—

Having moved in this category from desire to frustration and then to despair, this final poem constitutes a nadir for the poet-lover as she contemplates a tragic rejection by God himself. Not only is she denied human love, but, when she seeks consolation from the Divinity, He is effectually indifferent.

V *Marriage Poems*

The final category of love poems to be considered deals with the subject of marriage. Although Dickinson never married, she perceived the institution with her usual wit and insightful understanding from several points of view. First, a small group of poems treats marriage from the traditionally youthful and feminine perspective. These poems function as a kind of wish fulfillment for a young unmarried woman as they depict her desire for a conventional and idealized marriage. Typically, in such works as "Forever at his side to walk" (*P*, 246; I, 177), "Although I put away his life" (*P*, 366; I, 291–92), and "The World—stands—solemner—to me" (*P*, 493; I 375–76), the speaker longs to serve and attend to the wishes and needs of an imagined husband, to share in his trials and successes in this life, and finally to be glorified with him in the next.

A second and more important strain in her poetry considers marriage as a decisive and consequential act which marks the end of childhood and the beginning of maturity. In her often quoted poem, "I'm ceded—I've stopped being Their's," the poet contrasts baptism and marriage while emphasizing the transfiguring effects of both rituals upon the developing individual:

I'm ceded—I've stopped being Their's—
The name They dropped upon my face
With water, in the country church
Is finished using, now,
And They can put it with my Dolls,
My childhood, and the string of spools,
I've finished threading—too—

Baptized, before, without the choice,
But this time, consciously, of Grace—
Unto supremest name—
Called to my Full—The Crescent dropped—
Existence's whole Arc, filled up,
With one small Diadem.

My second Rank—too small the first—
Crowned—Crowing—on my Father's breast—
A half unconscious Queen—
But this time—Adequate—Erect,
With Will to choose, or to reject,
And I choose, just a Crown—

(*P*, 508; II, 389–90)

Baptism, which gave her a name and placed her officially in her parents' keeping, is identified with the time of her youth, with her dolls and her spools of thread. Now, she writes, she has "stopped being Their's"; she has "finished threading" and playing the part of a young girl. Another ritual, one associated with images of royalty, "Diadem," "Rank," and "Crown," is about to mark her maturity and bestow upon her another name, her "supremest name."

The contrast between the two rituals and the two conditions of her life is amplified when she writes that, as a child, she was baptized "without the Choice" and was heard crying on her father's breast; but this time, as a woman, she acts "consciously, of Grace," and stands "Adequate—Erect,/With Will to choose, or to reject." Using geometric imagery to describe the stages of development marked by the two rituals, she writes that she has been "Called to my Full—The Crescent dropped—/Existence's whole Arc, filled up." The image compares life to a circle in which baptism forms one crescent and in which marriage contributes the final arc which completes the circle. Blending religious ritual with coronation motifs, and highlighting the changes between youth and maturity, the poem stands as a remarkable artistic achievement that captures a woman's exuberant happiness as she contemplates the day of her marriage.

The same theme of marriage as fulfillment, as the achievement of status and maturity, finds a somewhat different treatment in another poem. In "I'm 'wife'—I've finished that—," the poet's mildly ironic handling of the female persona in the poem creates a counterpoint to the apparent declarative, assured, and quietly firm tone of the woman speaking:

> I'm "wife"—I've finished that—
> That other state—
> I'm Czar—I'm "Woman" now—
> It's safer so—
>
> How odd the Girl's life looks
> Behind this soft Eclipse—
> I think that Earth feels so
> To folks in Heaven—now—
>
> This being comfort—then
> That other kind—was pain—
> But why compare?
> I'm "Wife"! Stop There!
>
> (*P*, 199; I, 142–43)

The words " 'wife,' " and "Czar," and " 'Woman' " are equated in the first stanza to announce that, along with the institutional role of wife, a female achieves a level of privilege and recognition, as well as the final biological realization of her sex. By repeating the word "that" in "I've finished that—/That other state," the persona indicates a mild disdain for the girlhood she has left behind. However, the curious phrase, "It's safer so," is a bit of dramatic irony that lends a shade of shyness or fear to this woman who has been so confidently announcing in the first three lines her achievement and her new degree of power.

In the second stanza, the persona repeats that her condition feels different and that she is happy to have let go of her girlhood. She compares herself to those who, glorified in heaven, are looking back with wonderment and relief at the earth they left behind. In the final stanza she stops herself short of continuing the comparison between the two separate conditions of girlhood and marriage. She asserts with some smugness that it is not necessary to analyze and compare, since it is now more than enough to answer all questions by simply affirming that she is a wife.

Dickinson's poetic portrait of this woman who is so content to be a wife ironically reveals that the woman has a degree of self-assurance about herself and her condition that she really has not earned. Status has been conferred upon her, and she is unable to reflect upon it or to understand its real sources. The only sentence in the poem that reveals independent thinking on her part is "It's safer so," but that statement introduced an important qualification of her status that she did not pursue. And the poem ends with a determined reluctance to think ever again about her marital station. It is this blind, unthinking acceptance of role and value conferred upon it by society that Dickinson questions. Her irony, then, is not aimed at marriage so much as at the narrow complacency it creates in some women.

Her irony grows even stronger in "She rose to His Requirement." Using the same distinctions she had developed in the two previous poems between girlhood and maturity, Dickinson bitterly questions just what women are supposed to like about marriage:

> She rose to His Requirement—dropt
> The Playthings of Her Life
> To take the honorable Work
> Of Woman, and of Wife—
>
> If ought She missed in Her new Day,
> Of Amplitude, or Awe—
> Or first Prospective—Or the Gold
> In using, wear away,
>
> It lay unmentioned—as the Sea
> Develope Pearl, and Weed,
> But only to Himself—be known
> The Fathoms they abide—
>
> (*P*, 732; II, 558–59)

"His Requirement" dominates the opening stanza. The husband, who has not been mentioned in the two previous poems, is here depicted not as lover, companion, or friend, but as a standardbearer of excellence. She, who as a girl with her playthings, was beneath him, has risen to his expectations and can now take up "honorable Work" with the dual distinction "Of Woman, and of Wife." The irony is as blatant and biting in this stanza as in any Dickinson has ever written. Dickinson is clearly contemptuous of the enforced inferiority of women and of the fact that their value and individuality are recognized only in terms of the men they marry.

In the next two stanzas Dickinson reflects upon the disappointment or regret that a woman might feel about her role in marriage.

If her feeling of significance begins to fade, or if her happiness starts to wear thin, the wife has no recourse but to hide her discontentment like the sea that hides both pearl and weed. Stoically, she must endure with the knowledge that God alone perceives "The Fathoms they abide." This poem stands as one of the saddest portraits of human relationships that Dickinson ever drew.

From the idealistic wish that marriage would be a blissful dedication to another, to the view that it is a practical institution of ritualized maturation, to the grim fact that it can enslave women in positions of inferiority, Dickinson's vision of marriage, and finally of human love, encompassed all the possibilities. She was no cynic about love, as the search for it and final success with it in her own life reveals; but, much as she may have wished that all humanity might find peace and joy within each other's arms, she was too much of a realist, and too keen an observer of those around her, to believe that such an achievement was always possible.

CHAPTER 5

The Struggle for Sanity

A large number of poems by Emily Dickinson record with vividness and accurate detail a condition which a layman might simply consider as a nervous breakdown, but which a practicing psychologist might well see as symptomatic of the form of insanity that is labeled psychosis. These poems describe the great internal pain, tension, fear, and depression that result in a decisive and somewhat lasting mental disorientation or loss of the ability to perceive, reason, and function successfully within the realm of practical daily experience. The poems also indicate a knowledge of forces and motives beneath the conscious, working mind and an awareness that they may be the real guides and causes of human behavior. In addition, numerous complementary poems deal with the after effects of a breakdown or with a psychotic reaction, as well as with the efforts of adjustment and rehabilitation which follow a debilitating emotional upheaval.

As telling and as powerful as some of these poems are, few scholars have been willing to confront their meanings directly, and fewer have been willing to consider what the existence of these poems may indicate concerning the life and mind of Emily Dickinson. The possibility that she herself might have fully experienced the painful departure from reality that she describes in these poems has been either largely ignored or discounted. Until very recently, the tendency among biographers and scholars of the poet has been, in general, to regularize and normalize anything in her behavior that has appeared to be either odd or abnormal. Speaking of this defensive tendency among biographers of Dickinson, Anna Mary Wells has summarized it in a brief and challenging article: ". . . it seems curious that no biographer has ever discussed the possibility of mental illness as a causative factor in her eccentricity. It would almost appear that they have feared to do so, as if any implication that illness was involved in its production would somehow depreciate the poetry or as if our American self-image demanded that our literature as distinguished from that of Europe must be assertively healthy."[1] Whatever the cause among critics, whether a defensive love for the poet and her poetry or a sense of American chauvinism, they have tried to perpetuate the idea that there was nothing really irrational about her conduct or life-style. In fact, Millicent Todd Bingham gave voice to the position of most critics in her book *Emily Dickinson's Home* when she stated that one of her central objectives was to "replace queerness with reasonableness as an explanation of Emily Dickinson's conduct."[2]

Dickinson's complete withdrawal from society during her middle age and her refusal to see anyone, including old and dear friends, is a good case in point. Thomas H. Johnson, in his interpretive biography of the poet, has rationalized her withdrawal by emphasizing her superior nature: "Though one is tempted to find in the total retreat of her later years an element of the neurotic, the fact seems clear that she was possessed to a most uncommon degree by emotional responses so acute as to be painful to herself and others."[3] John Crowe Ransom agrees with Johnson's analysis: "Her sensibility was so acute that it made her excessively vulnerable to personal contacts. Intense feelings would rush out as soon as sensibility apprehended the object, and flood her consciousness to the point of helplessness." Ransom also justifies her withdrawal and her hiding of herself by asserting that she was practicing "economy," "frugality," and "renunciation"—as all poets must—in order to maintain the integrity of her soul for the sake of her poetry.[4]

Theodora Ward reinforced the theory of Dickinson's excessive sensitivity: "She lived so close to the center of her being, to the mainsprings of the life of spirit, that she brought to every contact an emotional charge and an enhanced awareness that made extraordinary demands on her store of vital energy." Because her responses to life involved every bit of her consciousness and tended to drain her of energy, Ward describes Dickinson's withdrawal as her "need of limiting her sources of stimulus." Despite such self-imposed limitations on life, Ward maintains that Emily Dickinson's "life was crowded with rich and varied experience."[5] Although it is difficult to perceive how she could have had such "rich and varied experience" shut away from most contacts with people, Allen Tate has also called her life "one of the richest and deepest ever lived on this continent."[6] Perhaps these critics mean that she had rich and varied "imaginative" experiences and that her "fantasy" life was the richest and deepest. Her life, on a mental level, was certainly superior to most; but, in terms of living experiences, in terms of real and continued contact with the forms, the events, and the people which account for the diversity of life, its richness and its complexity, her experiences were limited.

Finally, Charles R. Anderson, when speaking of her withdrawal from society, has observed that "the stages by which she became a recluse were so gradual . . . as to take much of the eccentricity out of such behavior." He then explains her seclusion and neutralizes its uniqueness by seeing it simply as an "extension of the clannish tendency in the Dickinsons" and as another version of "the artist's desire for privacy."[7]

However, a few critics have suggested the oddity of Emily Dickinson's withdrawal. Among them are John Malcolm Brinnin and Clark Griffith. Both make reference to her psychology, and both consider the possibility of an internal crisis as the causative factor. Brinnin admits that "Psychology may hold clues to great disparities among aspects of Emily Dickinson's personality," and he wonders what "emotional disaster it was that drove her to elect and finally to covet a life of obscurity."[8] Griffith, after noticing the fear and the emotional weakness involved in her choice to withdraw from society, declares that "There is the retreat backward into childhood, which is the crucial fact about Emily Dickinson's seclusion."[9]

Concerning the poems under consideration, critics have frequently misjudged their content by seeing them as symbolic accounts of other subjects such as physical pain, death, the problem of knowing, or the dichotomy of mind and body. Or, like David T. Porter, they have emphasized the created persona of the poet by insisting that the "I" voice in the poems is a poetic device or convention and is not the poet herself speaking.[10] But the majority of critics have not gone as far as Porter in separating the poet from the poetry. Writing in *The Voice of the Poet*, Brita Lindberg-Seyersted summarizes the opinion of most scholars on the subject: ". . . she expressed her thoughts, feelings and parts of her experience in her poems as she did in her letters, and with even greater frankness in the former. . . . we may infer that the poems are expressions of the poet herself, and even more fully and freely so than her letters." Finally, she writes, "In Emily Dickinson's case then it would seem a fallacious rigorousness to exclude all thought of a connection between the "I" of the poems and Emily Dickinson herself."[11]

Among critics who have accepted that the poetry more or less reflects and reorders the poet's own experience, a mixed and cautious attitude exists about the question of Dickinson's mental illness. Henry Wells admits that no explanation of her life "can keep us from feeling in the end that there was something a bit weird about her after all." He asserts, "To fail to recognize grave abnormality in Emily's life or at least the reflections of this condition in her poetry, constitutes a serious omission." But, despite this view, Wells regards her madness as closely allied to her artistic genius; in fact, he believes that her madness was the fuel for her genius and that her artistic creations were the cure for her madness. He concludes that she "outlived and outfought her madness."[12]

Theodora Ward recognizes that certain poems indicate a shaking of the foundations of her psychic being, but Ward is unable to admit that the poems indicate a real or complete breakdown. She writes: "The extraordinary clarity with which she was able to record the experience shows that she did not pass beyond the border of sanity, for the insane cannot explain themselves."[13] This assertion is not a valid justification for Dickinson's sanity since the insane can and often do explain themselves quite eloquently. In fact, numerous accounts exist that were written in the first person by the patients themselves who are describing their thoughts and feelings during and after a mental illness. Ward's statement indicates perhaps the misconceptions concerning mental illness which have prevented serious scholars from honestly considering what the lessons of modern psychology may offer by way of helping to understand the mind and soul of Emily Dickinson.

William R. Sherwood speaks of "defending" Dickinson's integrity and sanity, as if that were the function of scholarship. By reordering the sequence of the 1862 poems as formerly determined by the Johnson variorum edition, Sherwood intends to prove that "Emily Dickinson did not have a crack-up . . . but a conversion." Later, he lists with clear detail "the implications of modern psychology" for the Dickinson scholar; but, after he includes potential sources in her life of masochism, repression, and sublimation, he dismisses any insights they might suggest in favor of what "the devout would understand as the apprehension of the position death, suffering, and tantalizing uncertainty occupy in God's beneficent plan."[14]

Two important scholars, Clark Griffith and John Cody, are notable for their fairly comprehensive but theoretical reconstructions of Emily Dickinson's psychological life; and both firmly support the idea that she suffered some mental abnormality. Clark Griffith, relying especially on Freudian theory, believes she suffered from a poor relationship with her father which caused her to feel both fear and envy about masculinity, a hatred for the feminine side of herself, and a desire to retreat to the secure world of her childhood. Griffith finds that these concerns enter her poetry through repression and displacement and that they become generalized and projected onto her view of the world and thereby achieve a universality of statement about the suffering, fear, and insecurity experienced by all humanity. Furthermore, he believes that she in all probability did experience a nervous breakdown: "There is considerable evidence that at least once or twice during her life Miss Dickinson came close to the sort of mental crisis which her poetry describes. . . . these incidents have the sound of complete nervous exhaustion and perhaps even a brush with crackup."[15]

John Cody, a practicing American psychiatrist, has produced a psychograph of Emily Dickinson based upon psychological interpretations of her poems and letters and upon the comments and the observations made about her by her contemporaries. According to Dr. Cody, a deficient and unsatisfying childhood relationship with her mother damaged Dickinson's psychosexual development so that she grew up to be a woman fearful, helpless, and constricted. But these problems also led to a flowering of her poetic genius. As Dr. Cody summarizes her situation,

> Without such a mother Emily Dickinson could not have become the poet we know. It was Mrs. Dickinson's failure as a sufficiently loving and admirable developmental model that set in motion the series of psychological upheavals which were unmitigated misfortunes for Emily Dickinson *the woman.* These maturational impasses consigned her to a life of sexual bewilderment, anxiety, and frustration by impairing those processes of psychic growth which would have made the roles of wife and mother possible. With reference to Emily Dickinson *the artist,* one cannot speak of misfortunes at all. For, amazing as it may seem, Mrs. Dickinson's inadequacies, the sequence of internal conflicts to which they gave rise, and the final psychotic breakdown all conspired in a unique way to make of Emily Dickinson a great and prolific poet.[16]

In addition, Dr. Cody believes the years 1857 to 1864 were crucial ones in Dickinson's development. During this time her depression deepened, and her feelings of hopelessness and estrangement reached such severity that she suffered a psychotic episode. In the process of self-rehabilitation, which peaked during 1862, her poetic outpourings reached their greatest level.

In the light of Dr. Cody's work, it seems justifiable and wise to assert that a strong possibility exists that some form of mental illness affected the poet and that it should never be summarily dismissed in any discussion of her biography. The precise nature and degree of illness, the period of breakdown, and the specifics regarding causes and consequences, however, must remain theoretical as our understanding of the diseases of the human mind develops, and as we learn more about the relationship between creativity and madness. In addition, as long as the subject of an investigation cannot be examined, a gap in certitude seems impossible to avoid. Nevertheless, a critic's reluctance to deal with the themes of neurosis and breakdown because of fear about the negative reflection it may cast upon the poet now seems narrow and paternalistic. A close examination of a group of her poems about these themes reveals both a mature consciousness that is keenly sensitive of the fine line which separates sanity from insanity and a brave soul that is aware of the awesome struggle necessary to maintain a wholesome integrity.

I *The Breakdown*

Dickinson has written a number of poems which treat a specific point in time, a moment within a personal history when the mind collapses, suffers such a shattering strain and sense of disorientation that the person is never again able to percieve the world in the same way. As she describes the episode in one poem, a complete transformation of character occurs:

> And Something's odd—within—
> That person that I was—
> And this One—do not feel the same—
> Could it be Madness—this?
>
> (*P*, 410; I, 319)

The moment of breakdown, though sudden and irresistible, is the end product of a larger period of time in which the mind has gradually been undergoing a deterioration through tension, trouble, and trauma:

Crumbling is not an instant's Act
A fundamental pause
Dilapidation's processes
Are organized Decays.

'Tis first a Cobweb on the Soul
A Cuticle of Dust
A Borer in the Axis
An Elemental Rust—

Ruin is formal—Devils work
Consecutive and slow—
Fail in an instant, no man did
Slipping—is Crash's law.

(*P*, 997; II, 721)

Her household and garden images in the second stanza are excellent devices for suggesting the erosion of reason and spirit. Furthermore, they are subtle preparations for the image of the Devil which dominates the third stanza. A spider, spinning a cobweb on the soul, and a worm, eating through to the center of a life and mind, foreshadow the persistent, insidious ambitions of the Devil himself. Madness is, therefore, like possession.

Two other poems explore this sense of being trapped, of feeling helpless in the face of a consistent and inevitable deteriorating mental disease. "It knew no lapse, nor Diminution" makes use of legal terminology ("Diminution," "Dissolution," "Annulled," "Exchange") to emphasize the indifferent forcefulness of the disease:

It knew no lapse, nor Diminution—
But large—serene—
Burned on—until through Dissolution—
It failed from Men—

I could not deem these Planetary forces
Annulled—
But suffered an Exchange of Territory—
Or World—

(*P*, 560; II, 427)

The outcome is ironically understated: she suffers not a simple exchange of place but a serious transformation of her entire world.

"I saw no Way—The Heavens were stitched" uses cosmic imagery and pictures the depths of alienation by isolating the individual in an empty and indifferent universe:

I saw no Way—The Heavens were stitched—
I felt the Columns close—
The Earth reversed her Hemispheres—
I touched the Universe—

And back it slid—and I alone—
A Speck upon a Ball—
Went out upon Circumference—
Beyond the Dip of Bell—

(*P*, 378; I, 300)

One of the few critics who attempts an analysis of this poem maintains that the poet "found, not meaningless chaos, but a vision of the great wholeness of the universe."[17] However, it seems to me that the overwhelming sense of isolation and loneliness ("A Speck upon a Ball"), the feeling that one cannot reach a spiritual peace ("The Heavens were stitched"), nor ordinary reality ("Beyond the Dip of Bell") are the reactions of one who is not feeling the glory of a vision but experiencing the depths of despair.

In another poem a psychological collapse is rendered in images of a shipwreck:

A great Hope fell
You heard no noise
The Ruin was within
Oh cunning wreck that told no tale
And let no Witness in

The mind was built for mighty Freight
For dread occasion planned
How often foundering at Sea
Ostensibly, on land

The collapse of sanity is the sinking of "a great Hope," the secret, unobserved shattering of a dream or wish for a happy and ordered life. The second stanza offers opposing popular images for the mind. While humankind may believe the mind to be like a mighty freight train that is on solid ground and capable of handling great thoughts as well as great suffering, the mind is in reality like a foundering ship at sea which, when overburdened, is likely to sink.

The poem concludes with a stanza that suggests the condition of a living death:

> A closing of the simple lid
> That opened to the sun
> Until the tender Carpenter
> Perpetual nail it down—
>
> (*P*, 1123; II, 788–89)

For the one who has suffered a breakdown, there is a subsequent withdrawal from life and activity, an inability or fear or hatred of facing the day. This feeling of estrangement and isolation lasts, the poet tells us, until the moment of death when God will seal forever the eyes, the mind, and the coffin.

Several other poems give voice to this condition of life-in-death. Characteristically, it is a feeling of paralysis, of being turned to stone, and of feeling extreme cold and numbness. Poem 1046 opens with a shocking image for the loss of reason and then develops images of immobility through associations with sculpture:

> I've dropped my Brain—My Soul is numb—
> The Veins that used to run
> Stop palsied—'tis Paralysis
> Done perfecter on stone
>
> Vitality is Carved and cool.
> My nerve in Marble lies—
>
> (*P*, 1046; II, 739–40)

Her stillness, her inability to function, the poet suggests, is more than a human ailment subject to possible remedy. It is something which has transformed her into an object without feeling and beyond life itself. In anguish over her condition, she asks, "Who wrought Carrara in me/And chiselled all my tune."

In another poem, she reaffirms the fact that what she suffers from is not a disease in any ordinary sense, nor is it subject to healing through any known medicine. Her ailment can best be described as a form of petrifaction in which her spirit and her enthusiasm for life have been drained from her and replaced with a cold insensibility:

It knew no Medicine—
It was not Sickness—then—
Nor any need of Surgery—
And therefore—'twas not Pain—

It moved away the Cheeks—
A Dimple at a time—
And left the Profile—plainer—
And in the place of Bloom

It left the little Tint
That never had a Name—
You've seen it on a Cast's face—
(*P*, 559; II, 426–27)

In the first stanza there is an ironic use of the language of health and sickness. The poet assures us that, although medicine and surgery were not necessary, there was indeed sickness and pain—although of a different order. The next seven lines achieve a degree of intensity by focusing only on the face and by recording the changes that occur in its expression as a measure of withdrawal and alienation.

The language of health and sickness also informs "There is a Languor of the Life" (*P*, 396; I, 310–11); but, as in the previous poems, the emphasis is on the uncurable:

There is a Languor of the Life
More imminent than Pain—
'Tis Pain's Successor—When the Soul
Has suffered all it can—

A Drowsiness—diffuses—
A Dimness like a Fog
Envelops Consciousness—
As Mists—obliterate a Crag.

The images of enervation and stupor in this poem are the equivalent of the petrifaction, the paralysis, and the living death of the previous poems. After extreme and prolonged psychic turmoil, the poet says, one ceases to feel altogether, ceases to feel anything including pain. One is beyond pain and in a condition of complete numbness where all of one's perceptions have become clouded, inaccurate, and unresponsive. The second stanza is a reasonable description of a psychotic condition in which the mind is removed from reality and enters a deathlike inertia. The will is stifled ("A Drowsiness—diffuses"), and consciousness is so blurred that the sharp edges or hard facts of reality can no longer be perceived ("As Mists—obliterate a Crag").

The closing stanzas manifest the separation between the victim and his environment:

The Surgeon—does not blanch—at pain—
His Habit—is severe—
But tell him that it ceased to feel—
The Creature lying there—

And he will tell you—skill is late—
A Mightier than He—
Has ministered before Him—
There's no Vitality.

The victim's isolation from his world is capsulized in the surgeon's inability to help and in his observation that "skill is late." Not understanding the illness within, the surgeon considers the patient's withdrawal and his lack of feeling as indicative of death.

II *Three Poems*

Among her many poems which attempt to describe the condition of derangement, her most affecting ones have been those written in the first person which seem to describe the collapse as she herself lived through it. In addition to the poems already discussed in which the first person is used or implied, several others deserve special attention. "It would never be Common—more—I said" (*P*, 430; I, 333–34) is a statement of psychic biography in which Dickinson describes her mental life before and after the breakdown. As a young girl she is happy, full of love for the world, and outgoing:

I'd so much joy—I told it—Red—
Upon my simple Cheek—
I felt it publish—in my Eye—
'Twas needless—any Speak—

I walked—as wings—my body bore—
The feet—I former used—
Unnecessary—now to me—
As boots—would be—to Birds—

I put my pleasure all abroad—
I dealt a world of Gold
To every Creature—that I met—
And Dowered—all the World—

Then suddenly, for a reason which is unexamined in this poem, her life suffers a reversal; and all her joy and confidence in life vanish:

When—suddenly—my Riches shrank—
A Goblin—drank my Dew—
My Palaces—dropped tenantless—
Myself—was beggared—too—

In the next stanza, the least poetical one in the poem, which is written in five lines rather than in four and which lacks all rhyme, the discordance of her life is appropriately rendered in a discordant melody:

I clutched at sounds—
I groped at shapes—
I touched the tops of Films—
I felt the Wilderness roll back
Along my Golden lines—

The poem concludes with the bewildered poet asking plaintively for her lost sense of peace and contentment:

The Sackcloth—hangs upon the nail—
The Frock I used to wear—
But where my moment of Brocade—
My—drop—of India?

One of her greatest lyrics, "It was not Death, for I stood up," has been occasionally misunderstood as a poem dealing with something other than a serious psychic upheaval. Charles R. Anderson treats the poem as an expression of religious despair;[18] and John B. Pickard also treats the poem as if its subject were despair: "The pattern of the poem reflects the chaos of tortured emotions and the wretchedness of despair."[19] Clark Griffith, on the other hand, correctly discards despair as the subject "because, as the last line puts it, there are no hopes, no expectations of change or remission, through which a feeling of despair could be justified." He observes that the poem "turns out to be grounded in a psychic disturbance."[20] Because of the images and the sensations rendered in her other poems that deal with mental disturbance, Griffith's conclusion seems amply justified. In this poem the emphasis on inertia and withdrawal seems to be descriptive of a catatonic state:

> It was not Death, for I stood up,
> And all the Dead, lie down—
> It was not Night, for all the Bells
> Put out their Tongues, for Noon.
>
> It was not Frost, for on my Flesh
> I felt Siroccos—crawl—
> Nor Fire—for just my Marble feel
> Could keep a Chancel, cool—
>
> And yet, it tasted, like them all,
> The Figures I have seen
> Set orderly, for Burial,
> Reminded me, of mine—
>
> As if my life were shaven,
> And fitted to a frame,
> And could not breath without a key,
> And 'twas like Midnight, some—
>
> When everything that ticked—has stopped—
> And Space stares all around—
> Or Grisly frosts—first Autumn morns,
> Repeal the Beating Ground—
>
> But, most, like Chaos—Stopless—cool—
> Without a Chance, or Spar—
> Or even a Report of Land—
> To justify—Despair.
>
> (*P*, 510; II, 391–92)

The poem overwhelms the reader with alternatives and opposites. We sense that the poet is trying to describe an experience which she finds virtually indescribable. Although she cannot say just what it is, she can say what it is not and what it is like. Her subject, though clearly of an abstract nature, is rendered in metaphors of location and bodily sensation. We find in this poem many of the references and images that Dickinson has used in other poems to describe a breakdown—particular images of death, immobility, isolation, and coldness. Stanzas one and three invite comparisons of her condition with death and darkness. While she is alive and although it may be noon, her emotional dejection and feeling of estrangement from life preclude her perception of what is positive, bright, and uplifting.

In stanza two she describes the extremes and reversals of bodily temperature characteristic of her confused and imbalanced responses to life—at once full of a feverish nervousness and an icy immobility. Inner contradictions and reversals of perception stultify her spirit, constrain her will, and negate her sense of free choice in the fourth stanza. Stanza five, with its oppressive sense of isolation and death, acts as a coda to the last stanza in which the poet comes closest to describing her mental condition. It is "most, like Chaos," she writes, a state of disorder, formlessness, and infinite emptiness. The poem ends by depicting the soul as lost, as one beyond aid, beyond a realistic contact with its environment, beyond, even, despair.

Another great lyric which has been frequently misunderstood is "I felt a Funeral, in my Brain." Critics generally have considered the poem to be about either an actual funeral or a symbolic representation of suffering. Thomas H. Johnson and Richard Chase believe the poem presents a detailed view of a New England funeral service from the point of view of an acutely sensitive spectator—the poet herself.[21] John B. Pickard also believes the poem represents an actual funeral although perceived "through the ebbing sensations of a dead person."[22] On the other hand, William R. Sherwood and Charles R. Anderson read the poem as a metaphorical description of despair.[23] But, like the previous poem, the content of this one recreates a psychic breakdown or, as Clark Griffith states, "the onset and triumph of lunacy":[24]

I felt a Funeral, in my Brain,
And Mourners to and fro
Kept treading—treading—till it seemed
That Sense was breaking through—

And when they all were seated,
A Service, like a Drum—
Kept beating—beating—till I thought
My Mind was going numb—

And then I heard them lift a Box
And creak across my Soul
With those same Boots of Lead, again,
Then Space—began to toll,

As all the Heavens were a Bell,
And Being, but an Ear,
And I, and Silence, some strange Race
Wrecked, solitary, here—

And then a Plank in Reason, broke,
And I dropped down, and down—
And hit a World, at every plunge,
And Finished knowing—then—

(*P*, 280; I, 199–200)

The rituals of a New England funeral, as well as the anguish, regret, and feeling of loss associated with an actual burial, are internalized in the poet's mind. Because she feels as if something in her has died, the funeral image supplies her with a set of symbols to dramatize her loss. The poem describes the end of sanity, the loss of reason, relevance, and self-control within a formerly familiar environment.

The first two stanzas introduce the mounting pressure and tension that the speaker is undergoing just prior to a complete breakdown. The continual treading to and fro of the mourners in the first stanza is symptomatic of the growing confusion in her mind—of the rise in rigid, tedious, repetitive, and compulsive thinking. Line four suggests the breaking down she anticipates of all the ordinary and familiar patterns of her sense perceptions. Disorientation and compulsion are reinforced and heightened in stanza two by the relentless beating drum which threatens to paralyze or numb her mind completely.

In stanza three the coffin, symbol of her soul or rational faculties, is being readied for interment. The monotonous pounding of the leaden boots in the funeral procession recalls the mental anguish of the first two stanzas. Moreover, stanza four continues the funereal imagery by indicating that the death knell is tolling from the church bell tower. However, the sound of this bell, internalized and heightened as the whole cacophony of sounds are in this poem, suggests the total isolation of the poet from her world. The bell functions to deafen her to the various sounds and voices of her environment and to fill her mind with a single, shattering tone. In the final stanza, the separation from reality is confirmed when the scaffolding over the grave gives way and "a Plank in Reason, broke." The speaker falls into irrationality, thereby breaking all the ties that formerly bound her to the world, and ceasing, finally, all thought, perception, and understanding.

The poem achieves a degree of immediacy by taking the reader step by step through a richly symbolic vocabulary to the very brink of an experience which is virtually incommunicable. Unlike the previous poem, "It was not Death, for I stood up," which is discursive and descriptive, this poem achieves an objective correlative for relating the passage from rational control to irrationality.

III *Rehabilitation*

If, in fact, Emily Dickinson herself suffered in some degree the shattering nature of a mental breakdown as the number and quality of these poems seem to indicate, we have the poetry itself as evidence that she survived and resisted incapacitation and that she triumphed over her illness by turning her pain into song. Indeed, this process must have been neither a smooth nor an an easy one for her, nor could she expect special understanding or attention from those around her. Poor appetite, eye trouble, religious melancholia—these were the kinds of familiar problems that her family and her doctors were equipped to understand and succor. But serious mental illness, such as she describes, was not well understood in rural Massachusetts, nor were there adequate treatment facilities. In the mid-1840s, Dorothea Lynde Dix was able to get the asylum at Worcester expanded only because her saintly determination outlasted the protest and resistance of the legislators. For the most part, insane persons were the objects of ridicule or contempt and were kept locked behind bars, chained, and whipped into obedience. Even the commonest necessities were denied them, most of them lived in filth and misery, and many died as a result of their inadequate food, shelter, and clothing.

Emily Dickinson did not belong of course, in a madhouse; she was not so incapacitated that she was unable to make adequate adjustments on her own. Her therapy was self-inspired and pragmatic, and it achieved for her a kind of peace or resignation which allowed her to live out her life in creative pursuits. All the details of her adjustments and adaptations, of course, can never be known; but in such poems as "I breathed enough to take the trick" (*P*, 272; I, 194),

"After great pain, a formal feeling comes" *(P* 341; I, 272), "I tie my Hat—I crease my Shawl" *(P*, 443; I, 341–42), "There is a pain—so utter" *(P*, 599; II, 460), "From Blank to Blank" *(P*, 761; II, 579), and "As One does Sickness over" *(P*, 957; II, 693–94), she describes not only the necessity for perserverance but also how one may take some comfort in ritual and in a self-imposed regularity. To her, one could achieve a sense of order and meaning in life by acting as if order and meaning existed. One of her firmest beliefs in these poems is that, despite how one feels or thinks, one must still function. She admits such behavior is a difficult lie ("To simulate—is stinging work"), but it is essential "To hold our Senses—on" *(P*, 443; I, 342). We are impressed in these poems by her Herculean strength of character and by her remarkable will to live.

The fact that the poems themselves exist may be a direct consequence of her mental suffering. As Dr. Cody has written, "Psychological calamities, decades of frustration, isolation, and loneliness all created a void that Emily Dickinson's talent rushed in to fill. Without this void there might well have been no poet."[25] While the poems may be a product of personal tragedy, they in any case remain a testament to Emily Dickinson's ultimate triumph.

CHAPTER 6

The Secret and Spectacle of Nature

PERHAPS the favorite popular image of Emily Dickinson is drawn from the more than five hundred poems that she wrote on the subject of nature. Picturing her from one of her youthful poems as "The little Tippler," "Inebriate of Air," and "Debauchee of Dew—/Reeling—thro endless summer days—/From inns of Molten Blue" (*P*, 214; I, 149) is to see her as the elfin, carefree young girl who wanders through New England fields and woods and who has little to do but take delight in the beauty and magic of the preindustrial American landscape. The vision, of course, is less a real portrayal of the actual poet than a reflection of the longings of everyone for a carefree, innocent childhood, and for a time when our countryside was not blighted by factories, automobiles, and pollution. As a nature poet, Dickinson has written much that is in keeping with this image of her. A good deal of her nature poetry is sentimental and unaesthetic; it bluntly appeals to our commonest appreciation for gentle Mother Nature and for all her little creatures. But, Dickinson's finest nature poems—and there are many of them—reflect a unique understanding of the relationship between man and nature and express an appreciation for the beauty and variety of natural phenomena which goes beyond the obvious and the trite.

By 1860, nature as a literary subject had been a favorite among poets for more than a hundred years. From James Thomson and William Wordsworth, to William Cullen Bryant and Emerson, nearly every possible idea concerning nature had been expressed. Nature as the moral teacher, as the cure for the ills of civilization, as the analogy for what is divine, as the promise for immortality—all had been stated and so restated that a fresh approach to nature was fast approaching an impossibility. Added to this situation was the fact the poets who lacked the vision and the skill of a Wordsworth or an Emerson simply mouthed ideas concerning nature that they had not created or experienced for themselves; and, as a result, a deluge of mawkish sentimentality replaced genuine feeling. Nature as a subject of literary investigation was soon to slip, therefore, into the realm of the stylized, the conventional, and the dull. At her worst, Dickinson is subject to this decadence; but her general skepticism about the relationship between man and nature, her acute observations and concern for precise detail without becoming scientifically analytical, her interest in natural subjects usually thought of as unsuitable for poetry, and her poetic experimentations in rendering man's perception of natural phenomena make her status as a nature poet unquestionably original and important.

There are three general categories of attitude in her nature poetry. The first—and the minor one,—she shares in common with her romantic and transcendental contemporaries and predecessors who believed that a mystical bond exists between man and nature and that nature reveals to man things about mankind and the universe. The second and most important and philosophically challenging category is antitranscendentalist, for she declares that an unbreachable separation exists between man and nature and that nature is at the core indifferent toward the life and interests of mankind. The third and by far the largest category, occupying a kind of philosophical middleground between the opposing first and second categories, affirms the sheer joy and the appreciation that she feels in the variety and spectacle of nature.

I *Transcendental Visions*

The poems in the first category are in general halfhearted restatements of transcendental notions regarding nature. Usually weak poems with an amateurish ring to them, they lack the complexity and craftsmanship of image and structure we associate with Dickinson's finest work; and their mediocrity probably confirms our view that the transcendental doctrines did not satisfy her deepest level of questioning concerning nature. For example, "The Murmur of a Bee" is an overly structured poem which repeats a single stanzaic form three times with almost an exact replication throughout of phrasing, rhyme, and meter:

> The Murmur of a Bee
> A Witchcraft—yieldeth me—
> If any ask me why—

'Twere easier to die—
Than tell—

The Red upon the Hill
Taketh away my will—
If anybody sneer—
Take care—for God is here—
That's all.

The Breaking of the Day
Addeth to my Degree—
If any ask me how—
Artist—who drew me so—
Must Tell!

(*P*, 155; I, 111–12)

In each stanza a notion typical among the transcendentalists is bluntly stated. In the first stanza we see their deep respect for the mystery ("Witchcraft") of nature. In her saying that it would be easier to die than to explain why she perceives this mystery, she is affirming their belief that wisdom through nature is somehow mystically perceived and is therefore virtually inexpressible in words. The second stanza announces the surrender of one's ego in the presence of nature and that all things divine can be found in nature. The last stanza confirms that contact with nature improves the mind and heart of the individual.

The ideas found in these last two stanzas had become prosaic maxims for the poet who was writing about nature in 1860, although they are in fact faint echoes in condensed form of several sections of Emerson's monumental essay, *Nature*, published in 1836, which had been the most thorough transcendental treatment of the theory of nature. Dickinson's poetic rendition of them is a far cry from their original vitality, and it reveals her lack of conviction in their applicability. For example, the following brief passage often quoted from Emerson's essay is both a more poetic and a more sincerely felt version of the ideas found in the second stanza of the above poem: "Standing on the bare gound,—my head bathed by the blithe air and uplifted into infinite space,—all mean egotism vanishes. I become a transparent eyeball; I am nothing; I see all; the currents of the Universal Being circulate through me; I am part or parcel of God."[1]

In another early poem, "The Skies can't keep their secret!" (*P*, 191; I, 137–38), the poet contrasts a mystical intuition about nature with the scientific desire to know precisely. In the first two stanzas she is sure that a great and important secret exists in nature; and she playfully suggests that she might be made privy to it if only she were clever enough to bribe the mystery from one of nature's creatures. But she dislikes the analytical approach and decides "It's finer—not to know—/If Summer were *an Axiom*—/What sorcery had *Snow?*" She prefers the anti-intellectual approach to nature which will keep its magical quality fresh for her and prevent a reduction of all phenomena to a simplistic set of axioms.

Perhaps Dickinson's best poem in this category is " 'Nature' is what we see"; and its debt to Emerson's essay is so great that it prompted Jack L. Capps in his study, *Emily Dickinson's Reading 1836–1886*, to conclude, "The metaphors of this poem are a list of favorite Emerson subjects."[2]

"Nature" is what we see—
The Hill—the Afternoon—
Squirrel—Eclipse—the Bumble bee—
Nay—Nature is Heaven—
Nature is what we hear—
The Bobolink—the Sea—
Thunder—the Cricket—
Nay—Nature is Harmony—
Nature is what we know—
Yet have no art to say—
So impotent Our Wisdom is
To her Simplicity.

(*P*, 668; II, 515)

In the first two stanzas (the poem is divided into three quatrains although they are not printed separately), the poet is trying to define nature in terms of externals—what we can see and hear of it. In both stanzas she manages to suggest the totality of nature by selecting elements representative of land, sea, and sky, and of the large and the small. Also, we are made aware of the poet's frustration in seeking a definition of nature through her negations in the last lines of both stanzas and through her substitutions of seemingly larger, more comprehensive terms for our experience of nature—"Heaven" for what we see, and "Harmony" for what we hear. The use of "Heaven" is perhaps meant to suggest that nature is not only beautiful to look at but is also the source of divine inspiration. "Harmony" implies not only orderly and pleasing sound but also unity among its various elements with man. In the last stanza she reaches her most comprehensive definition of nature when she affirms that nature is knowledge itself which surpasses our ability to express.

The familiar Emersonian notions of nature as the great teacher and as the source of beauty and moral wisdom are echoed in this poem. However, Dickinson's comment in the closing two lines of the poem modifies, perhaps unintentionally, the apparent direction of the poem. Instead of concluding the poem with some sense of resolution or satisfaction in having approached the meaning of nature, she hedges at the last and offers doubt concerning our actual ability to appreciate nature genuinely or to act upon her lessons. Nature, she concludes, is essentially simple despite its outer manifestations of multiplicity. Yet, our minds are unable to bring into a cohesive whole the disparate stimuli experienced by our senses. Her struggle, then, to define nature in transcendental terms is not altogether a successful one. In its conclusion the poem points in the direction of a different attitude toward nature which Dickinson could find intellectually acceptable even if less comforting.

II *Inscrutable Nature*

A second category of poems reveals a point of view which challenged and contradicted what had become traditional romantic values regarding nature. Since her goal had never been to write a complete philosophy of nature, these poems cannot be made to show a systematic or progressive mode of thinking. They do show, however, an active and original mind—one which would not be satisfied with an easy generalization or with a platitudinous idea. Her sharp observation of things as they are, her wit, her courage, and her unquenchable need to experience the truth regardless of authority and custom, make these poems unique in pre-Darwinian America.

A brief poem which embodies her controversial line of thought contains a phrase which is unusually modern in tone:

A little Madness in the Spring
Is wholesome even for the King,

But God be with the Clown—
Who ponders this tremendous scene—
This whole Experiment of Green—
As if it were his own!

(*P*, 1333; III, 921)

The poem is an affirmation of the ecstasy one feels in the spring and of the salutary benefits derived from releasing oneself from one's usual manner and routine in order to revel in the seasonal rebirth of the earth. But there is a difference established in the poem between this healthy "Madness" on the one hand, and foolishness on the other. "God be with the Clown," she writes, who believes nature can be possessed by man, or understood and rendered in terms of what is human. She warns that it would be ridiculous to make the joy that one feels in the spring cause for believing that one therefore understands nature. The leap from feeling to presumed knowledge is one that she recognized as absurd.

The key to her idea lies in the phrase "Experiment of Green." Commenting on this word "Experiment," Charles R. Anderson has written, "So the traditional doctrine of nature as a finished creation, whether bequeathed or revealed to man, is replaced by a word with scientific overtones, suggesting that nature is a process by which essential truths are searched out and proved in particular experiments."[3] The experimental quality in nature makes all conclusions about it hypothetical and tentative, and subject to examination. It is the way the modern age feels about nature, and our science has taught us that the best we may do is to think in terms of mere probabilities regarding nature. She must have felt something close to this view, for the same idea finds succinct expression in this little poem:

Experiment escorts us last—
His pungent company
Will not allow an Axiom
An Opportunity.

(*P*, 1770; III, 1184)

Unlike other nature poets who might permit their feelings to lead to their faith, Dickinson never abandoned her clear-eyed observation aided by reason. In a clever quatrain, she put it this way:

"Faith" is a fine invention
When Gentlemen can *see*—
But *Microscopes* are prudent
In an Emergency.

(*P*, 185; I, 134)

Dickinson's desire for intellectual assurance that was independently achieved kept her back, as we have seen in Chapter 2 of this work, from a commitment to Christ. We see the same toughness of mind as her nature poems refuse what would be unconfirmed though comfortable assertions.

Dickinson believes that a separation exists between the world of nature and that of man. We live outside of nature and are permitted to observe it, experience it, and enjoy it if we can; but we are not privileged to enter into its secret. To express this idea, she used the analogy of a traveling circus in one poem:

We spy the Forests and the Hills
The Tents to Nature's Show
Mistake the Outside for the in
And mention what we saw.

Could Commentators on the Sign
Of Nature's Caravan
Obtain "Admission" as a Child
Some Wednesday Afternoon.

(*P*, 1097; II, 771)

Nature is a spectacle, she says, and we judge wrongly if we believe its meaning may be gleaned from simply viewing its outward show. We are like the children who mistakenly believe the excitement of going to the circus is watching the big tents go up. What is more, as much as we may wish to enter and learn of nature from "behind the scenes," we cannot gain admittance.

A more thorough statement of this idea is found in the following poem which is both playful and serious:

What mystery pervades a well!
That water lives so far—
A neighbor from another world
Residing in a jar

Whose limit none have ever seen,
But just his lid of glass—
Like looking every time you please
In an abyss's face!

The grass does not appear afraid,
I often wonder he
Can stand so close and look so bold
At what is awe to me.

Related somehow they may be,
The sedge stands next the sea—
Where he is floorless
And does no timidity betray

But nature is a stranger yet;
That ones that cite her most
Have never passed her haunted house,
Nor simplified her ghost.

To pity those that know her not
Is helped by the regret
That those who know her, know her less
The nearer her they get.

(*P*, 1400; III, 970–71)

The well is a fact of nature, and it serves in this poem also as a symbol for the whole mysterious realm of nature. Just as the poet cannot see the bottom of the well, she likewise cannot see to the hidden meaning of nature.

The second stanza sharpens the analogy. The well, like nature, appears to have no limit; it can be viewed only on its surface. Furthermore, the use of the word "abyss" to describe the depth of the well in the last line of the second stanza implies a certain fear and awe in her response to the overwhelming remoteness and inaccessibility of nature. In contrast, the grass in the third stanza is not afraid of the well, nor is the sedge in the fourth stanza fearful of the bottomless sea. They, unlike the poet, are part of nature; therefore, they share in its secret with confidence.

The fifth stanza comes bluntly to the point that man and nature are strangers. Those poets and writers who claim to know nature and speak freely and often about it, Dickinson maintains, have never really gained admittance to nature's house nor analyzed its spirit: they are like the children in the previous poem who mistake the outward show of tent-raising for the actual circus. In the sixth stanza, Dickinson suggests in a cryptic way what it is about nature that makes it awesome and unknowable. Richard Chase's comment on this stanza points precisely to the problem as Dickinson conceived it: "We cannot know nature by getting close to it, because the closer we get to nature the closer we get to unconsciousness and death."[4] She was aware that the real mystery of nature is that of existence itself. While nature may give her occasional joys, it in the last analysis reminded her of the impermanence of things and of her own mortality. For Dickinson, when an individual became a part of nature, when he entered the "haunted house," he was going to meet his death.

When another romantic poet, such as Walt Whitman, contemplated this merge with nature, he was not likely to be awestricken and fearful. He tended to perceive it in optimistic terms as part of the gentle and orderly process of life. Whitman writes: "I bequeath myself to the dirt to grow from the grass I love,/If you want me again look for me under your boot-soles."[5] His corpse, placed in the ground, enters the process of nature and becomes renewed: he grows again as grass. Whitman affirms this relationship between nature and death, and he finds unity and immortality awaiting him. Dickinson, on the other hand, is unsure of immortality and suspicious of nature, and is unwilling to believe and affirm what she cannot test for certain; she will allow herself, at best, only cool skepticism.

Among the few things that she had some measure of certainty about was Nature's cosmic indifference not only toward man but within the realm of its own creatures. A short poem written late in her life treats nature's indifference with a heavily ironic tone:

Apparently with no surprise
To any happy Flower
The Frost beheads it at its play—
In accidental power—
The blonde Assassin passes on—
The Sun proceeds unmoved
To measure off another Day
For an Approving God.

(*P*, 1624; III, 1114)

A murder is described in the poem, and everyone involved in it—the victim, the assassin, and the witness—are completely unconcerned about it. Without intent to kill, the frost, quite by accident, beheads a flower in full bloom, and then simply continues on its way. The happy flower is apparently neither surprised nor upset by this sudden and mortal interruption in its life cycle. Watching from above, the sun, who might have prevented the crime had he been shining, continues in his daily course uninvolved and uninterested in what occurs below. There is an apparent conspiracy of silence and indifference toward the random, unplanned, yet cruel happenings in nature. And overseeing it all is the most disturbing element in the entire scheme—a God who gives his approval to it.

The poem is objective and dispassionate in its choice of language and imagery, but the irony is unmistakable. The episode is condensed with brilliant economy and precision, and no sentimentality or didacticism creates a human analogy. A lesser poet could easily bemoan the sudden death of a person who, like the happy flower, was taken in the full blossoming of his days. But Dickinson's intention is larger. Her comment, concealed within the poem's metaphor, charges that nature is, to the bewilderment of man and the will of God, without motivation and conscience. In the implied larger sense of the poem, it stands as a challenge to any writer who would employ the pathetic fallacy or who would blend in a transcendental reverie the three separate worlds of man, nature, and God.

That nature would either reflect one's mood or help to heal and improve one's mood when one was troubled or suffering were other assumptions held by nature poets which Emily Dickinson challenged. In "I dreaded that first Robin, so," nature in gay springtime array neither reflects nor assuages the inner pain of the speaker. To the contrary, nature threatens the poet with additional suffering because of its mindless indifference to human needs:

> I dreaded that first Robin, so,
> But He is mastered, now,
> I'm some accustomed to Him grown,
> He hurts a little, though—
>
> I thought if I could only live
> Till that first Shout got by—

Not all Pianos in the Woods
Had power to mangle me—

I dared not meet the Daffodils—
For fear their Yellow Gown
Would pierce me with a fashion
So foreign to my own—

I wished the Grass would hurry—
So—when 'twas time to see—
He'd be too tall, the tallest one
Could stretch—to look at me—

I could not bear the Bees should come,
I wished they'd stay away
In those dim countries where they go,
What word had they, for me?

They're here, though; not a creature failed—
No Blossom stayed away
In gentle deference to me—
The Queen of Calvary—

Each one salutes me, as he goes,
And I, my childish Plumes,
Lift, in bereaved acknowledgment
Of their unthinking Drums—

(*P*, 348; I, 278)

The poet dreads nature, fears being mangled, pierced, and insulted by its untimely flourishing. She wishes to hide from the spring; or, better yet, she wishes the spring would not arrive. But nature is a process—orderly, unstoppable, and irreversible. Spring arrives on time and parades itself before her loudly and unthinking. We do not know what the poet's hurt is, but we know that it is of such severity that she compares herself to the suffering mother of Christ ("Queen of Calvary"). While nature may not be the cause of her pain, we are made aware that it will in no way help to ease her pain; nature will, in fact, contribute to her pain despite the poet's pleas to the contrary.

Another poem, "A Bird came down the Walk" (*P*, 328; I, 261), focuses on the separation between the worlds of man and nature, and it also develops the theme of nature's indifference by including other questions of fear and struggle. The first two stanzas are full of precise and picturesque detail:

> A Bird came down the Walk—
> He did not know I saw—
> He bit an Angleworm in halves
> And ate the fellow, raw,
>
> And then he drank a Dew
> From a convenient Grass—
> And then hopped sidewise to the Wall
> To let a Beetle pass—

The poem's quick trimeter line, varied by one tetrameter line in each stanza, is a suitable match for the sudden and irregular movements of a bird that is hopping along the ground. The bird's morning meal of worm and dew is, of course, quite natural; but the stress placed upon "raw" by setting if off with commas in the rhyming position emphasizes the unpleasant aspects of the feeding habits of a creature customarily pictured as harmless. His suddenly courteous behavior toward the beetle in stanza two conceals the struggle among nature's creatures for survival that we witnessed in the first stanza.

In stanzas three and four the bird's mood of fear and danger is increased with the intrusion of the poet:

> He glanced with rapid eyes
> That hurried all around—
> They looked like frightened Beads, I thought—
> He stirred his Velvet Head
>
> Like one in danger, Cautious,
> I offered him a Crumb
> And he unrolled his feathers
> And rowed him softer home—

The bird is suddenly alert to an unexpected danger, and he hurriedly looks around with wide open eyes. When the poet reveals herself, and through a gesture of kindness tries to participate in the life of the bird, she is repulsed; and the bird flies away. The attempt at rapprochement with nature fails.

The first line of the fourth stanza is in a curious position because it seems to apply to both the bird and the poet. The obvious reading of the line is that "the bird stirred his head like one in danger," and then the last word in the line, "Cautious," is meant to modify the "I" in the next line. However, the poet, having just witnessed the bird eat a raw worm, might have some fear of being bitten when she offers the bird a crumb that is on the tip of her finger. In this case the whole line could also refer to the poet. It would be in keeping with Dickinson's sense of economy and use of highly compressed language to have the line working in both ways at the same time.

This element of fear suggested in the above poem as a response to nature's threatening aspects is enlarged upon in another poem, "I started Early—Took my Dog" (*P*, 520; II, 399–400). Although the poem has received a variety of rich interpretations by scholars who have worked with the image of the sea as a symbol for either death or love or sexuality, the poem remains significantly interesting as a complex evaluation of mankind's relationship to nature.[6] As Clark Griffith has described it, the poem "constitutes, at bottom, a savage and a terrifying indictment of Nature."[7]

The first two stanzas open the poem in a lighthearted mood that suggests either a fairy tale or a romantic celebration of childhood's love of nature:

> I started Early—Took my Dog—
> And visited the Sea—
> The Mermaids in the Basement
> Came out to look at me—
>
> And Frigates—in the Upper Floor
> Extended Hempen Hands—
> Presuming Me to be a Mouse—
> Aground—upon the Sands—

The presence of mermaids and frigates with extended hands and the picture of the sea as a house with basement and upper floors combine to create that sense of the fantastic and the familiar present in most fairy tales. The frank innocence of the young girl is reflected in her unassuming and playful responses to what she sees in nature.

But this sweetness and tranquillity of a visit to the seashore is suddenly reversed in the next three stanzas:

But no Man moved Me—till the Tide
Went past my simple Shoe—
And past my Apron—and my Belt
And past my Bodice—too—

And made as He would eat me up—
As wholly as a Dew
Upon a Dandelion's Sleeve—
And then—I started—too—

And He—He followed—close behind—
I felt His Silver Heel
Upon my Ancle—Then my Shoes
Would overflow with Pearl—

The sea turns suddenly hostile, begins to menace the young girl, and molests her in strongly sexual terms, reaching from her foot to waist to bosom. When she flees, he pursues, continues grasping for her ankle, and offers her an ambiguous compensation of a shoe full with pearls. Curiously, the tone of these stanzas remain as gay and frolicsome as the opening two. The little girl, whose voice we hear, does not seem as astonished by what's happening to her as we perhaps are. This device of the child persona, which is at work in many other poems, cunningly separates the poet from her poem. Affording Dickinson a mask to hide behind, the persona allows her in this poem to speak with impunity against the imponderable foe, nature.

By the last stanza, the persona is safe at home, back in the world of man:

Until we met the Solid Town—
No One He seemed to know—
And bowing—with a mighty look—
At me—The Sea withdrew—

The "Solid Town" of man stands in sharp contrast to the flowing, amorphous world of nature symbolized by the sea. Where the town offers safety, security, and strength, the sea can only bring the instability of change and process. Arrogant and sinister to the last, the sea bows in a haughty fashion and withdraws. Beyond a deceptively simple format and playful ambiguity, the poem implies a dreadful fear of nature. Dickinson subtly accuses nature of threatening to obliterate the identity and sanctities of man. In even a casual contact with nature, the risks involved demand images of violation, engulfment, and drowning. As in other poems of this category, death—actual or symbolic—is the legacy of nature.

III *The Pageantry of Nature*

Although Emily Dickinson may have philosophically despaired at times of ever understanding nature, of knowing the secret ties that bind man and the natural world together, of experiencing a oneness and wholeness with nature, she was capable of feeling and of expressing that great sense of joy and transport which accompanies an artist's loving appreciation for the external beauty of nature. A third category of her nature poetry—by far the largest in number, accounting for at least four-fifths of all her nature poetry—expresses with loving detail and emotional genuineness the numerous forms and characteristics of the natural environment. These poems, unaffected by and large by intellectuality and philosophical speculation, range from the simple sketches of flowers, birds, and insects, to the fully detailed portraits of summer storms, the changing seasons, the sunrise and the sunset. Although not all of these poems exhibit the level of artistry of her best work, most of them are characterized by keen perception, witty analysis, and salutary intent. A number of them are minor masterpieces that are noted especially for their striking imagery, experimental quality, or succinctness of expression.

The daily drama of sunrise and sunset was an attractive subject for many poems. Her perspective is that of the painter, delighting in the visual charms of color and texture, and occasionally describing the scene with reference to terminology drawn from the painter's art:

> A slash of Blue—
> A sweep of Gray—
> Some scarlet patches on the way,
> Compose an Evening Sky—
>
> (*P*, 204; I, 144–45)

She was apparently conscious of trying to imitate in poetry what the painter tried to capture on canvas; for, in another poem in which she awkwardly attempts to describe the sunset through a series of color-drenched portraits of the surrounding landscape, she concludes the poem with reference to Renaissance painters whose sky-scrapes were stylized and uninspired:

> These are the Visions flitted Guido—
> Titian—never told—
> Domenichino dropped his pencil—
> Paralyzed, with Gold—
>
> (*P*, 291; I, 210)

Like Guido Reni, Titian, and Domenichino, artists who were unable to render the sunset on canvas because its beauty and its color overwhelmed their mimetic abilities, her attempts at capturing in language the essential beauty and the grandeur of the sunset are necessarily weak and imprecise.

Color dominates another awkward attempt at rendering the sunset in a poem which begins, "Whole Gulfs—of Red, and Fleets—of Red—/And Crews—of solid Blood—/Did place about the West—Tonight—" (*P*, 658; II, 507). In a better poem filled with color, "She sweeps with many-colored Brooms," the quaint image of a speedy but careless housewife who is earnestly trying to tidy up the heavens serves as the spirit of the evening sky. Like an artist with a paint-filled brush, she leaves strips and drops of color wherever she swings her broom:

> She sweeps with many-colored Brooms—
> And leaves the Shreds behind—
> Oh Housewife in the Evening West—
> Come back, and dust the Pond!
>
> You dropped a Purple Ravelling in—
> You dropped an Amber thread—
> And now you've littered all the East
> With Duds of Emerald!
>
> And still, she plies her spotted Brooms,
> And still the Aprons fly,
> Till Brooms fade softly into stars—
> And then I came away—
>
> (*P*, 219; I, 157)

Two final poems about the sun's movement are remarkable for their unique imagery. The first, "I'll tell you how the Sun rose" (*P*, 318; I, 242), uses a series of domestic images coupled with action verbs to render the spreading and then receding rays of sunlight. The rays of the morning sun unravel like decorative ribbons from a lady's sewing box; the color of the morning sky drenches the town so that the church steeples appear to swim in amethyst. The imagery for the setting sun blends the dominant shades of purple and yellow by picturing yellow children who are climbing a purple stile. Finally, as the last gray lights of day fade into darkness, the image of "A Dominie in Gray" who is leading the bright children away closes the poem.

The second poem opens with an arresting conceit of beauty and intensity:

> Blazing in Gold and quenching in Purple
> Leaping like Leopards to the Sky
> Then at the feet of the Old Horizon
> Laying her spotted Face to die.
>
> (*P*, 228; I, 163)

There is an interplay of the sun's heat, color, and movement captured in the opening two lines and intensified by the image of the mighty leopard. His gold body with dark spots leaping across man's field of vision is a vivid analogy of the majesty and grandeur of the sun's passage across the sky. The poem closes by referring to the sun as the "Juggler of Day," an apt image for the sun's ability to suspend and rotate planets throughout the universe in seeming defiance of the laws of gravity.

Like the daily cycle of sunrise and sunset, the larger seasonal cycles of the year became the subject for her poetry. Each season is examined for its unique beauty, and often for its mysterious connection with other seasons. In winter, despite the snow and cold, there is the hidden promise of spring and of the full blossoming and warmth of summer; likewise, in the colorful harvest of autumn is the prospect of returning to the barren frost of winter.

Spring is a favored season, and it always draws from Dickinson an excitement and a sense of the promise hidden in all things. As she plainly describes her reactions in one poem, "I cannot meet the Spring unmoved" (*P*, 1051; II, 741). The emphasis is on resurrection in "A Lady red-amid the Hill" (*P*, 74; I, 59–60) and the buried bud of life which soon will blossom into the lily. As might be expected, the religious connotations of spring are never far from her mind. In another poem she writes that "Spring is the Period/Express from God" (*P*, 844; II, 637). Though He may be found in other seasons, the poem affirms that, during the spring, "None stir abroad/Without a cordial interview/With God."

From the local-color sketches of spring in "An altered look about the hills" (*P*, 140; I, 99–100), she moved to an examination of spring which emphasized its position as part of an eternal cycle in "New feet within my garden go" (*P*, 99; I, 77). The opening stanza reflects upon what is new about spring:

> New feet within my garden go—
> New fingers stir the sod—
> A Troubadour upon the Elm
> Betrays the solitude.

The poet's garden is rejuvenated and stirs with the appearance of squirrels, worms, and birds. But, in the last stanza, she is reminded that, despite this apparent show of new life and beauty, the dead still lie beneath the ground and the snows of winter will just as surely fall again. Her enthusiasm is necessarily modified, and she closes the poem by referring to the spring with the sobering epithet of "pensive."

Her best attempt at describing the elusive beauty of the spring is found in "A Light exists in Spring" (*P*, 812; II, 613). The poet attempts to describe the apparent glow or coloration in the environment which indicates that spring has arrived, but she admits that the actual nature of this light is elusive and cannot be understood by science:

> A color stands abroad
> On Solitary Fields
> That Science cannot overtake
> But Human Nature feels.

The light of spring cannot be grasped by science because it affects our intuition, not the rational or pragmatic sides of our nature. The middle stanzas explore the mystical quality of this light which enlarges our perception with spiritual understanding. In the last stanza the poet states the significance of her experience by drawing an analogy with the sense of desolation which follows the departure of a religious experience:

A quality of loss
Affecting our Content
As Trade had suddenly encroached
Upon a Sacrament.

Harsh reality intrudes upon the illumination of an early spring day just as the impersonal, materialistic concerns of "Trade" intrude upon the ceremony and spirituality of a sacrament. The poem closes by affirming the spiritual rejuvenation of spring although it be short-lived or interrupted.

Although the summer was her favorite season of the year, she never successfully rendered its special atmosphere and beauty in her poems. An early attempt, "A something in a summer's Day," succeeds in suggesting that there is something wonderful and indescribable about summer, although what it could be is only vaguely hinted at:

A something in a summer's Day
As slow her flambeaux burn away
Which solemnizes me.

A something in a summer's noon—
A depth—an Azure—a perfume—
Transcending ecstasy.

And still within a summer's night
A something so transporting bright
I clap my hands to see—

(*P*, 122; I, 88)

Another early attempt, "The Gentian weaves her fringes," mourns the passing beauty of summer with a mock-heroic sermon, a funeral, and a burial service which are attended by some of her favorite summer creatures—the bobolink, the bee, and the butterfly among others. The poem ends with an often quoted, playfully pantheistic blessing:

In the name of the Bee—
And of the Butterfly—
And of the Breeze—Amen!

(*P*, 18; I, 20–21)

A much later poem on the same subject, "As imperceptibly as Grief," is stately, quiet, and dignified. In contrast to the previous poem, the drama of summer's departure is understated; and the poet's sense of loss seems more genuinely felt. Instead of a ceremonious observance celebrating the end of summer, this poem attempts to describe that subtle changes that occur during the last days of summer, ones which indicate the impending change of seasons:

As imperceptibly as Grief
The Summer lapsed away—
Too imperceptible at last
To seem like Perfidy—
A Quietness distilled
As Twilight long begun,
Or Nature spending with herself
Sequestered afternoon—
The Dusk drew earlier in—
The Morning foreign shone—
A courteous, yet harrowing Grace,
As Guest, that would be gone—

(*P*, 1540; III, 1060–61)

The sense of estrangement is deepened through the simile of a house guest who has stayed for a time gaining our love but who finds it impossible to remain. The guest's behavior remains courteous, but he grows ever more withdrawn and restless. Finally, "without a Wing/Or service of a Keel," the summer, dissolving into an idea, is gone with no apparent means of transport.

There are several poems on the autumn which are pleasant and picturesque renditions of the local scenery. One of the most engaging is an early poem which displays a droll sense of humor toward the season and the self:

The morns are meeker than they were—
The nuts are getting brown—

The berry's cheek is plumper—
The Rose is out of town.

The Maple wears a gayer scarf—
The field a scarlet gown—
Lest I should be old fashioned
I'll put a trinket on.

(*P*, 12; I, 15)

Lest she appear out of step with the new fashion of displaying color, she concludes, she should herself wear a bit of bright jewelry. This simple gesture of personal adornment is noteworthy because it is one of the very few instances in Dickinson's poetry where we witness her assent to what might have been termed in the nineteenth century a traditionally feminine practice.

Her finest poem about the transitional season of autumn, "These are the days when Birds come back" (*P*, 130; I, 92–93), focuses on what is popularly known as Indian summer—those occasional days that follow the first frosts of late autumn but which, because of their warm and hazy weather, remind one of early summer. Within her probing of the unusual appearance of Indian summer, she speculates as to whether it prefigures death or immortality in a poem divided into three sections of two stanzas each. In the first section the physical appearance of the season is described:

These are the days when Birds come back—
A very few—a Bird or two—
To take a backward look.

These are the days when skies resume
The old—old sophistries of June—
A blue and gold mistake.

The stanzas are linked through their identical opening phrases, "These are the days when." Although there is no scientific evidence for believing the birds actually return from their southern homes, the image is meant to convey how the few hardy breeds which do remain later than usual take advantage of the mild climate and make themselves conspicuous. The sky appears bright and blue as it did in June, although the use of the words "sophistries" and "mistake" indicate that the similarity cannot be trusted and needs further investigation.

In the next two stanzas her distrust is strongly verbalized, and the speciousness of the season is exposed:

> Oh fraud that cannot cheat the Bee—
> Almost thy plausibility
> Induces my belief.
>
> Till ranks of seeds their witness bear—
> And softly thro' the altered air
> Hurries a timid leaf.

She refers to the season as a "fraud" that cannot fool the sharp-eyed realist, the bee. She admits that she was sorely tempted to believe in a renewed summer until she saw the "ranks of seeds" and "a timid leaf" fall to the ground, for they assured her that this season was indeed autumn. However, the image of the seeds that bear witness to the death of a particular plant also suggests a promise of rebirth and an immortality for the species.

The concluding section of the poem develops the implicit religious imagery which surrounds this symbol of rebirth and immortality:

> Oh Sacrament of summer days,
> Oh Last Communion in the Haze—
> Permit a child to join.
>
> Thy sacred emblems to partake—
> Thy consecrated bread to take
> And thine immortal wine!

After reasoning as an adult from the evidence of the season and concluding that the season is a fraud, she leaps to the realization that only by abandoning her doubts and by becoming as a child again can she hope to see the emblematic meaning hidden in the season and partake of immortality. The poem ends, therefore, expressing not so much a commitment as a wish to believe and be blessed with life after death.

The winter did not hold much attraction for Emily Dickinson although she did write two imaginative poems about winter snowstorms, "It sifts from Leaden Sieves" (*P*, 311; I, 231–32), and "Like Brooms of Steel" (*P*, 1252; III, 868). Mostly she dreaded the winter and all that it symbolized for her. In the deepest part of a long New England winter, spring and the joy of living may be virtually unimaginable. Surrounded by ice and snow, working hard to keep warm through long evenings and short days, thoughts filled with depression and death readily surface. In a remarkable poem, "There's a certain slant of light," she recreated the sense of intolerable isolation and affliction that can accompany the long winter season:

There's a certain Slant of light,
Winter Afternoons—
That oppresses, like the Heft
Of Cathedral Tunes—

Heavenly Hurt, it gives us—
We can find no scar,
But internal difference,
Where the Meanings, are—

None may teach it—Any—
'Tis the Seal Despair—
An imperial affliction
Sent us of the Air—

When it comes, the Landscape listens—
Shadows—hold their breath—
When it goes, 'tis like the Distance
On the look of Death—

(*P*, 258; I, 185)

Like the poem on the mystical illumination of spring, "A Light exists in Spring," this poem focuses on the paradoxical light of winter which, instead of brightening the soul, darkens it and threatens the soul's sense of faith. Gloom pervades the poem, and the weight of it is conveyed through the exact rhymes as well as the language itself: "oppresses," "Heft," "Hurt," "Scar," "Despair," "affliction," "look of Death." But the affliction is not only oppressive, it is also impressive. It is a "Heavenly Hurt," and the words "Seal" and "imperial" lend a majestic, awesome quality to it. The suffering weighs one down, yet it is also ennobling. The winter, like death itself, affirms the uniqueness of our humanity at the same time that it threatens to take it away through trial and denial.

Dickinson's poems about storms and sudden summer rains are among her most dramatic and occasionally most playful. In "A Drop fell on the Apple Tree" (*P*, 794; II, 600), for instance, a summer shower is described in extravagantly imaginative terms. The light raindrops are said to be kissing the eaves and making the gables laugh, while the rest of them "went out to help the Brook/That went to help the Sea." At this point in the poem, she has a magical, childlike vision of raindrops: "Myself Conjectured were they Pearls—/What Necklaces could be—". The poem continues to record how the birds, the bushes, and the breezes all rejoice in the gently refreshing rain until the sun shows itself again and brings an end to the festivities.

The same light tone governs another poem about a more violent storm. "The Wind begun to knead the Grass" uses domestic images, touches of local color, and an array of action verbs to render the excitement of a rainstorm:

> The Wind begun to knead the Grass—
> As Women do a Dough—
> He flung a Hand full at the Plain—
> A Hand full at the Sky—
> The Leaves unhooked themselves from Trees—
> And started all abroad—
> The Dust did scoop itself like Hands—
> And throw away the Road—
>
> (*P*, 824; II, 624–25)

As the thunder gossips low, and as the lightning does a country jig in the air, the villagers, the birds, and the cattle hurry to their shelters. Finally, the waters "wreck" the sky, and lightning "quarters" a tree, but the poet observes with humor and mock innocence that somehow the storm "overlooked my Father's House."

Although she may have been inclined to treat storms with a certain casual playfulness, she was also capable of enlarging her theme to include suggestions of terror, awe, and destruction. For example, imagery of cosmic upheaval seems to inform the next poem:

> There came a Wind like a Bugle—
> It quivered through the Grass
> And a Green Chill upon the Heat
> So ominous did pass

We barred the Windows and the Doors
As from an Emerald Ghost—
The Doom's electric Moccasin
That very instant passed—
On a strange Mob of panting Trees
And Fences fled away
And Rivers where the Houses ran
Those looked that lived—that Day—
The Bell within the steeple wild
The flying tidings told—
How much can come
And much can go,
And yet abide the World!

(*P*, 1593; III, 1098)

The situation in this poem is much more threatening than in the previous poems, and the threat is enhanced by faint biblical allusions to the Day of Judgment. The wind seems to come from the outer reaches of the universe, and the simile of a bugle gives the suggestion that it is being blown by Gabriel himself. The synesthetic image of a "Green Chill" that ominously passes is metamorphosed into a figure of death, an "Emerald Ghost," against whom people must lock their windows and doors. Death is present again in the image for lightning, "Doom's electric Moccasin," which arrives with the stealth of an Indian. The bell that wildly rings in the church steeple suggests both death and a time for final reckoning. In the end, however, the poem does not make conclusive use of the doomsday imagery; the poem returns to the real storm and ends with a commonplace.

Although she loved flowers and had knowledge regarding them, her poems on flowers are not distinctive. She wrote more poems about her favorite, the rose, than any other flower; but most of these poems are usually conventional and sentimental. A poem about the arbutus is typical of the best of them; and, although it begins with the sharp detail and freshness of language that distinguishes her finest work, it quickly fades into cliches and the superficial:

Pink—small—and punctual—
Aromatic—low—
Covert—in April—
Candid—in May—
Dear to the Moss—

Known to the Knoll—
Next to the Robin
In every human Soul—
Bold little Beauty
Bedecked with thee
Nature forswears
Antiquity—

(*P*, 1332; III, 920

Bees and birds were among her favorite creatures in nature, and she wrote a few of her best genre portraits about them. Her caricature of the bee's appearance, his incessant activity, and his monotonous buzzing are wittily charming and graceful:

Bees are Black, with Gilt Surcingles—
Buccaneers of Buzz.
Ride abroad in ostentation
And subsist on Fuzz.

Fuzz ordained—not Fuzz contingent—
Marrows of the Hill.
Jugs—a Universe's fracture
Could not jar or spill.

(*P*, 1405; III, 975)

Bees are whimsically pictured as swashbuckling pirates fancily dressed in black and gold who swagger across the countryside while plundering and looting treasures that Dickinson describes, in a novel metaphor, as "Marrows of the Hill." But this pretentious image of them is punctured by the alliterative pattern of the letter "B" in the first two lines and by the rhyming of "Buzz" and "Fuzz" which approximates the sound they make. After all, they are only little bees, and their booty is just pollen.

Her skill at burlesque is continued in the second stanza in which she contemplates their food ("Fuzz") on a mock metaphysical level. "Fuzz ordained—not Fuzz contingent" is a sophisticated scholastic distinction to simply affirm that their food is essential to their nature. The concluding hints of universal destruction humorously extends the vital importance of honey to the order and stability of nature.

This poetic device of describing something little in language that is suggestive of issues and situations that are large is one she has successfully employed in other poems about the bee. "Did the Harebell loose her girdle" (*P*, 213; I, 149) and "A Bee his burnished Carriage" (*P*, 1339; III, 925) describe the simple gathering of nectar in terms of seduction and courtly love. "Of Silken Speech and Specious Shoe" (*P*, 896; II, 660), "His Feet are shod with Gauze" (*P*, 916; II, 671), "Like Trains of Cars on Tracks of Plush" (*P*, 1224; III, 852), and "His little Hearse like Figure" (*P*, 1522; III, 1049) are other poems which render the bee's appearance and activity in a playfully burlesque fashion.

Although many of her poems on birds do not refer to specific species by name, she has written exuberant portraits of the oriole, "One of the ones that Midas touched" (*P*, 1466; III, 1015–16); the bluejay, "No Brigadier throughout the Year" (*P*, 1561; III, 1074–75); the robin, "The Robin is a Gabriel" (*P*, 1483; III, 1025); and the bobolink, "The Way to know the Bobolink" (*P*, 1279; III, 889–90). Perhaps her most famous portrait is that of the humingbird:

> A Route of Evanescence
> With a revolving Wheel—
> A Resonance of Emerald—
> A Rush of Cochineal—
> And ĕvery Blossom on the Bush
> Adjusts its tumbled Head—
> The mail from Tunis, probably,
> An easy Morning's Ride—
>
> (*P*, 1463; III, 1010)

Critics who have commented about this poem have found it useful to compare it to an earlier poem on the same subject, "Within my Garden, rides a Bird" (*P*, 500; II, 383–84). This earlier poem is discursive, more literal, and much longer, since it consists of twenty lines. The images of the revolving wheel and of the nodding flowers are present in the earlier poem, but there is the added presence of the poet's dog and of several laborious and awkward figures of speech, including a cliché drawn from fairy tales. "A Route of Evanescence," then, has been regarded as an illustration of Dickinson's celebrated ability to economize and to condense her diction and her imagery when she is writing at her best.

The poem has also been justly praised for its achievement in rendering not merely a portrait of the bird but also the *impression* of the hummingbird upon the intellect; that is, the reader is invited to contemplate the hummingbird as the poet herself experienced it in a single fleeting instant of consciousness. Hence, with the opening series of rapid, synesthetic phrases, she emphasizes the sudden motion, the vibrating sound, and the iridescent color of the hummingbird as one might actually perceive it. Details about the garden setting, the name of the bird and even a statement of the fact that it is indeed a bird being described are all omitted in this concentrated account of specific sensuous detail.

The dominant impression of the hummingbird is its amazing speed that causes it to seemingly appear and disappear simultaneously. Therefore, the language of motion controls the images in the poem. "A Resonance of Emerald" suggests that sound and sight merge in one fleeting sensation because the bird moves so fast. "A Rush of Cochineal" emphasizes that even its brightest color can be only fleetingly grasped. The bird is no sooner perceived than it is gone, and the blossoms' nod of affirmation is all that remains to confirm that a hummingbird was indeed there. The closing lines fancifully suggest the bird's ability to speed easily from the remotest corner of the earth.

The final grouping of nature poems to be considered probably constitutes Emily Dickinson's most distinctive exploitation of nature's forms. Turning away from the traditional and the popular in nature poetry, she focused her attention upon the neglected oddities of nature—upon the life forms usually considered ugly, unpoetic, or unworthy of a writer's serious attention, such as the rat, fly, snake, worm, frog, spider, caterpillar, mushroom, bat, beetle, cricket, mouse, squirrel, and weeds. As Charles R. Anderson describes her achievement with this novel approach, it "made her nature poetry the beginning of a new mode rather than the end of an old one."[8]

In "The Rat is the concisest Tenant," Dickinson seems to challenge the conventional romantic response to nature by finding something for the reader that is acceptable and admirable about a rodent that is usually scorned as repulsive. She presents him as an integral part of nature:

> The Rat is the concisest Tenant.
> He pays no Rent.
> Repudiates the Obligation—
> On Schemes intent

Balking our Wit
To sound or circumvent—
Hate cannot Harm
A Foe so reticent—
Neither Decree prohibit him—
Lawful as Equilibrium.

(*P*, 1356, III, 937)

Instead of portraying the rat as scorned by civilization, she presents him as one who scorns civilization because of its reliance upon the laws of property. He is "concisest," terse, and succinct toward man, occupying little room for which he will not pay rent. We cannot understand him, nor can we affect him ("Hate cannot harm/A Foe so reticent"). Although he is beyond our understanding of usefulness and "Decree," she affirms that he deserves his part in the scheme of things and remains "Lawful as Equilibrium."

A more disturbing investigation of one of nature's poetically neglected species is "A narrow Fellow in the Grass" (*P* 986; II 711–12). In this poem Dickinson examines the fascination and fear that a snake can inspire in its onlookers. At first, the snake is observed for his strange beauty and behavior. His appearance is said to be "sudden"; and, wherever he moves in a field, "The Grass divides as with a Comb." His spotted body is given a degree of regal power when he is described as "a Whip lash/Unbraiding in the Sun." Yet, a disturbing undertone is present in the snake's hidden and unpredictable slithering movements. The biblical associations of the snake with evil are hinted at in the snake's fondness for empty, unpleasant places ("a Boggy Acre/A Floor too cool for Corn").

The last two stanzas contrast the poet's love for other parts of nature with the terror she feels toward the snake:

Several of Nature's People
I know, and they know me—
I feel for them a transport
Of cordiality—

But never met this Fellow
Attended, or alone
Without a tighter breathing
And Zero at the Bone—

The striking image at the close of the poem renders a feeling for the absolute horror and terror she experiences when she meets the snake. Constricted breathing and a bone-numbing chill are aspects of the paralyzing dread that the snake inspires. From an interested fascination for the creature, the poem develops the snake's associations with an evil power that threatens at the last to restrict man's freedom and dignity.

It seems fitting to close with one of her most profound and complex observations about nature. Her meditations upon the cricket in "Further in Summer than the Birds" has received perhaps more criticism and controversy than any other of her poems without any clear statement emerging as to its full philosophical import. The poem transforms the cricket's song through religious imagery and terminology to a momentous celebration that marks the poignant change of summer to winter, of life to death:

Further in Summer than the Birds
Pathetic from the Grass
A minor Nation celebrates
Its unobtrusive Mass.

No Ordinance be seen
So gradual the Grace
A pensive Custom it becomes
Enlarging Loneliness.

Antiquest felt at Noon
When August burning low
Arise this spectral Canticle
Repose to typify

Remit as yet no Grace
No Furrow on the Glow
Yet a Druidic Difference
Enhances Nature now.

(*P*, 1068; II, 752)

The crickets become active much later in the summer than the birds, and their dull chirring in the tall grass awakens in the poet thoughts of the season's impending end. She equates the crickets' performance to the celebration of a Mass hidden from her eyes and also from her understanding. Gradually the monotonous sound of the crickets' celebration casts her into a pensive mood and enlarges in her the feeling of loneliness.

By the third stanza, the ancient service performed by crickets since the beginning of time summons a consciousness of death in the poet, a feeling for the impermanence of all things. She refers to the Mass now as a "spectral Canticle," the purpose of which is to prefigure "Repose." "Repose" refers to the rest which follows at the end of activity; but, in the terms of this poem, as Charles R. Anderson has suggested, the nature of this rest is ambiguous: "Is this 'repose' the changelessness of eternity or the long sleep of winter?"[9] Are the crickets celebrating the life everlasting which man craves after death, or merely the end of existence within the natural order? As always, we have difficulty in finding dogmatic answers in Dickinson's greatest lyrics; and the last stanza remains sufficiently suggestive to prevent a positive categorization.

The first two lines of the fourth stanza indicate that, despite the "spectral Canticle," there has been no diminution of grace or beauty, "No Furrow on the Glow." The lively spectacle of summer still remains. Nevertheless, the poem concludes, nature has been enhanced with a "Druidic Difference." Is "Druidic" meant to refer to a pagan nature rite of the declining year, or to a magical and primitive joy in the continuity and wholeness of nature's promise? An explicit answer seems impossible, and perhaps one was never intended by the poet. As do so many of her great poems, this one sustains an articulated awareness of the inscrutable. The poem does not offer a lesson or an answer but simply an insightful grasp of the mystery of existence. The end of summer, of life, indicates a change which the crickets foretell in their Mass. But what that change consists of is beyond the poem; it is hidden in nature away from the poet's, and our, eyes.

CHAPTER 7

The Prose of a Poet

ALTHOUGH Emily Dickinson lived most of her life in the seclusion of her father's house, physically hidden from the eyes and ears of her contemporaries, the world was never far from her mind and from her word as the more than one thousand letters she wrote to family, friends, and mentors indicate. What she may have lost in the spontaneity and warmth we associate with lively human exchange, she made up for with a deepened verbal precision and psychological investment. In some cases, she was able to carry on a more enriching emotional communication through the mail than many of us are able to do in our more immediate face-to-face contacts. She seemed to thrive on the power of the disembodied idea, on the essence of a mind captured on paper and unencumbered by matter. As she wrote of this fascination to Higginson. "A Letter always feels to me like immortality because it is the mind alone without corporeal friend. Indebted in our talk to attitude and accent, there seems a spectral power in thought that walks alone" (*L*, II, 460).

That the writing and the receiving of letters were important to her is reflected in her verse. In poem 441 she announces, "This is my letter to the World," equating her poems to intimate, private messages addressed to "Sweet-countrymen" (*P*, 441; I, 340). The two versions of poem 494, "Going to Him! Happy letter!" and "Going-to-Her!" 494; I, 376–77), describe the joy, as well as the toil and occasional frustrations which the devoted letter writer experiences. Another poem, "The Way I read a Letter's—this, " memorializes the acute joy of reading mail; and it is especially interesting because of the unabashed peek it gives the reader into the poet's life:

The Way I read a Letter's—this—
'Tis first—I lock the Door—

And push it with my fingers—next—
For transport it be sure—

And then I go the furthest off
To counteract a knock—
Then draw my little Letter forth
And slowly pick the lock—

Then—glancing narrow, at the Wall—
And narrow at the floor
For firm Conviction of a Mouse
Not exorcised before—

Peruse how infinite I am
To no one that You—know—
And sigh for lack of Heaven—but not
The Heaven God bestow—

(*P*, 636; II, 489)

The details of the poem are delicately drawn, but they are so intimate as to be mildly embarrassing. The sensitive reader might almost feel the odd sensation that he is suddenly snooping into a private and sacred ritual in the poet's life.

I *The Art and Aim of Letter Writing*

The complex satisfactions gained from letter writing are largely lost in our present age of instant electronic communication with its frequent propensity for fragmented and perfunctory messages. In the past, letter writing was an art; and Emily Dickinson's methods of writing were perhaps even more consciously artistic than those belonging to many of her correspondents. Her letters were creations, some of which might begin to take shape years before they were mailed. David Higgins, in his useful study of her prose, describes the "scrap basket of Emily's workshop" discovered after the poet's death, which consisted of hundreds of scraps and drafts of prose and poetry in various stages of development.[1] Frequently, these were simply phrases and sentences jotted down as they occurred to her during her household routines. Some received further development when she returned to them during her free time, while others remained in their embryonic form on the backs of grocery lists and on the torn corners of used envelopes. This storehouse of expression she dipped into for her letters: "When she wrote letters she chose appropriate fragments and worked them into her prose. Sometimes the letter as a whole would pass through two or more drafts before it satisfied her. Meantime she would have chosen poems from the scrap basket or from her 'packets' and fitted them also into her letter. The final writing—the letter her correspondent actually received—might look spontaneous, but it was the last of several creative stages."[2]

Another aspect of her art reveals how conscious she always was of her audience, trying to send to her correspondents what best fitted their minds and needs. To dull friends, she sent prosaic messages; to those whom she thought would be appreciative, she sent poems, aphorisms, and the brilliant though frequently oblique flashes of insight she was capable of. She also "posed" herself for various members of her audience. Her stance is not only reflected in the tone of the letters—playful, childishly inquisitive, imperious—but in their signatures—"Emilie," to friends with whom she shared certain sentimentalities; "Your Scholar," to Higginson from whom she sought advice and encouragement concerning her poetry; and "Rascal," to Samuel Bowles, an old and intimate friend.

For most of her contemporaries, letter writing was merely one avenue of social communication, usually supplementary to the main business of a relatively active social life. But, for Dickinson, letters had become her single chosen method of association with others which permitted her not only to have harmonious communication with those she cared about but also to control the forms and degrees she wished her relationships to have. Her correspondence permitted her to exchange a mutual interest with someone without also having to endure either the requirements of genteel New England hospitality or the searching eyes of people in the flesh. For she was, for whatever complex set of reasons, painfully shy. In a letter to Mr. and Mrs. E. J. Loomis she verbalized the need to hide by quoting a passage from Genesis: "In all the circumference of Expression, those guileless words of Adam and Eve never were surpassed, 'I was afraid and hid Myself' " (*L*, III, 847). Richard Chase has succinctly summarized the several motives at work in Dickinson's letter writing: "Letters were, indeed, a form of magic by which Emily Dickinson could control her friends, could keep them at a suitable distance and in a certain relationship to her. They were the power by which she gained emotional and intellectual support in return for the devotion she offered, along with her aphorisms, her jokes, her news, and her profound thoughts."[3]

Since she invested so much of herself in her letters, she desired letters sent in return which displayed the same deliberate care and attention, an expression of mutual investment of feeling and will. And she could take offense at failures in this regard. When Mrs. J. G. Holland once made the mistake of sending one letter addressed to both Emily and Lavinia Dickinson, Emily sent this cutting reply:

> A mutual plum is not a plum. I was too respectful to take the pulp and do not like a stone.
>
> Send no union letters. The soul must go by Death alone, so, it must by life, if it is a soul.
>
> If a committee—no matter. (*L*, II, 455)

II *Poetic Prose*

The relationship between Emily Dickinson's prose and her poetry is a significant one. Not only did she include many poems in her letters, but her prose is so poetic at times that it is difficult to distinguish it from her poetry. As Milton Hindus has rightly observed, "Poets like Dryden and Coleridge left their poetry behind in their verse when they entered the strict portals of prose, but Emily brought all of her paraphernalia with her."[4] In fact, some of her prose can actually be divided into lines of regular meter which usually rhyme. A random search by John Tyree Fain of the 1894 edition of Dickinson's letters led to his discovery of a number of passages which fall into obvious verse patterns:

> "Then will I not repine/knowing that bird of mine,/though flown,/learneth beyond the sea/melody new for me,/and will return." (Letter of 1853; 162)

> "Affection is like bread,/unnoticed till we starve,/and then we dream of it,/and sing of it,/and paint it,/when every urchin in the street/has more than he can eat." (Letter of 1874; 276)

> ". . . could we see all we hope,/or hear the whole we fear/told tranquil, like another tale,/there would be madness near." (Letter of 1874; 278)

> "The slips of the last rose/or summer respose/in kindred soil/with waning bees for mates./How softly summer shuts,/without the creaking of a door,/ abroad for evermore." (Letter of 1880; 286)

". . . there is another sky,/ever serene and fair,/and there is another sunshine,/though it be darkness there;/never mind faded forests, Austin,/ never mind silent fields—/*here* is a little forest,/whose leaf is ever green;/ here is a brighter garden,/where not a frost has been;/in its unfading flowers/I hear the bright bee hum;/prithee, my brother,/into *my* garden come!"[5]

It would seem to hold true, as George Frisbee Whicher has said, that "Only a sentence or two and she was singing."[6]

But the relationship between her prose and poetry is more intrinsic than a similarity in sound pattern, for the best of both share a unique premise concerning language and thought. As David Higgins describes their similarity, "In both she tried to condense thought to its essence in epigram, trusting her reader to solve the puzzling paradoxes and puns and ambiguities along the way."[7] Typical examples of these characteristics may be drawn from a single letter addressed to Mrs. Holland in 1866:

After you went, a low wind warbled through the house like a spacious bird, making it high but lonely. When you had gone the love came. I supposed it would. The supper of the heart is when the guest has gone.

Shame is so intrinsic in a strong affection we must all experience Adam's reticence. I suppose the street that the lover travels is thenceforth divine, incapable of turnpike aims.

That you be with me annuls fear and I await Commencement with merry resignation. Smaller than David you clothe me with extreme Goliath.

Friday I tasted life. It was a vast morsel. A circus passed the house—still I feel the red in my mind though the drums are out. . . .

The lawn is full of south and the odors tangle, and I hear today for the first the river in the tree.

You mentioned spring's delaying—I blame her for the opposite. I would eat evanescence slowly. . . .

"House" is being "cleaned." I prefer pestilence. That is more classic and less fell. . . .

A woman died last week, young and in hope but a little while—at the end of our garden. I thought since of the power of death, not upon affection, but its mortal signal. It is to us the Nile. (*L,* II, 452–53)

Like much of her poetry, this letter is a dense collection of aphoristic phrases, oblique syntax and terminology, and difficult references. We sense a mind at work which responds to experience on many levels at once and is capable of vast leaps in thought through analogy.

One of Dickinson's favorite techniques was to include poetry in the body of a letter. To Higginson and to her sister-in-law, Sue, the poetry was usually included on separate sheets of paper. But in writing to her other correspondents, in order to fit a particular occasion or to express a certain feeling, she would frequently adapt a stanza or more of her poetry with usually a sentence or two of prose by way of a preface. In a letter to Louise and Frances Norcross, a love poem became a hymn to spring:

> Infinite March is here, and I "hered" a bluebird.
> Of course I am standing on my head!
> Go slow, my soul, to feed thyself
> Upon his rare approach.
> Go rapid, lest competing death
> Prevail upon the coach.
> Go timid, should his testing eye
> Determine thee amiss,
> Go boldly, for thou paidst the price,
> Redemption for a kiss.
>
> (*L*, II, 523)

In a letter to Edward S. Dwight, Dickinson adapts the last stanza of another love poem, "There came a day at summer's full," to serve as a tribute to the memory of Mrs. Dwight, whose picture Dickinson had just received from the bereaved husband:

> Again—I thank you for the face—her memory did not need—
>
> Sufficient troth—that she will rise—
> Deposed—at last—the Grave—
> To that *new* fondness—Justified—
> by Calvaries of love—
>
> (*L*, II, 389–90)

A poem on immortality serves as an excuse for not seeing Professor Joseph K. Chickering when he expressed his wish to call on her:

> I had hoped to see you, but have no grace to talk, and my own Words so chill and burn me, that the temperature of other Minds is too new an Awe—

We shun it ere it comes,
Afraid of Joy,
Then sue it to delay
And lest it fly,
Beguile it more and more—
May not this be
Old Suitor Heaven,
Like our dismay at thee?

(*L*, III, 758)

On occasion, Dickinson would enclose little more than a line or two of prose to accompany a whole poem to friends and members of the family as gifts or as expressions of love and remembrance. For example, "The Zeroes—taught us—Phosphorous" was included along with her brother's letter to Samuel Bowles (*L*, II, 426); during two separate bouts with illness, Ned Dickinson received, "A Field of Stubble, lying sere" (*L*, II, 577), and "The Bible is an antique volume" (*L*, III, 732); and, as a New Year's greeting, Mrs. Edward Tuckerman was sent "A Route of Evanescence" (*L*, III, 655).

Other characteristics of the letters that relate to certain oddities of her prose style might finally be mentioned. She had a propensity for using the subjunctive mood, as she did in much of her poetry; and she decorated her letters with archaisms and localisms such as "a'nt" for "isn't," and "he don't" and "eno." Her desire to express the essence of her thought caused her to usually pare away all that was superfluous in prose, including the usual connectives. However, the unique style of the letters is less a mark of a self-conscious prose writer's desire to appear unique than of a genuinely original mind whose thoughts and sensibilities demanded a mode of self-expression that was as compact and dramatic as her poetry.

When considering some of Dickinson's greatest letters, we find it difficult to agree with Henry W. Wells's evaluation that her letters were in "grey, everyday tones."[8] The following letter, as a case in point, is a lively, colorful narrative of the fire which destroyed part of the business center of Amherst on July 4, 1879:

We were waked by the ticking of the bells,—the bells tick in Amherst for a fire, to tell the firemen.

I sprang to the window, and each side of the curtain saw that awful sun. The moon was shining high at the time, and the birds singing like trumpets.

Vinnie came soft as a moccasin, "Don't be afraid, Emily, it is only the fourth of July."

I did not tell that I saw it, for I thought if she felt it best to deceive, it must be that it was.

She took hold of my hand and led me into mother's room. Mother had not waked, and Maggie was sitting by her. Vinnie left us a moment, and I whispered to Maggie, and asked her what it was.

"Only Stebbin's barn, Emily;" but I knew that the right and left of the village was on the arm of Stebbin's barn. I could hear buildings falling, and oil exploding, and people walking and talking gayly, and cannon soft as velvet from parishes that did not know that we were burning up.

And so much lighter than day was it, that I saw a caterpillar measure a leaf far down in the orchard; and Vinnie kept saying bravely, "It's only the fourth of July."

It seemed like a theatre, or a night in London, or perhaps like chaos. The innocent dew falling "as if it thought no evil," . . . and sweet frogs prattling in the pools as if there were no earth.

At seven people came to tell us that the fire was stopped, stopped by throwing sound houses in as one fills a well.

Mother never waked, and we were all grateful; we knew she would never buy needle and thread at Mr. Cutler's store, and if it were Pompeii nobody could tell her.

The post-office is in the old meeting-house where Loo and I went early to avoid the crowd, and—fell asleep with the bumble-bees and the Lord God of Elijah.

Vinnie's "only the fourth of July" I shall always remember. I think she will tell us so when we die, to keep us from being afraid.

Footlights cannot improve the grave, only immortality.

Forgive me the personality; but I knew, I thought, our peril was yours.

(*L*, II, 643–44)

The letter is full of interesting details, observations, and reactions. The reader can almost have the sense of being a part of the action. The vision of the caterpillar's measuring a leaf, the sound of the frogs' croaking in the ponds, and even the phrasing of "fell asleep with the bumble-bees and the Lord God of Elijah" constitute part of the magic which lend a rich, spirited vitality to the narrative.

Neither is there anything "grey" about the next letter, which is a vivacious and witty description of early spring sent to her Norcross cousins, Louise and Frances:

I think the bluebirds do their work exactly like me. They dart around just so, with little dodging feet, and look so agitated. I really feel for them, they seem so tired.

The mud is very deep—up to the wagons' stomachs—arbutus making pink clothes, and everything alive.

Even the hens are touched with the things of Bourbon, and make republicans like me feel strangely out of scene.

Mother went rambling, and came in with a burdock on her shawl, so we know that the snow has perished from the earth. Noah would have liked mother. . . .

Pussy has a daughter in the shavings barrel.

Father steps like Cromwell when he gets the kindlings.

Mrs. S[weetser] gets bigger, and rolls down the lane to church like a reverend marble. (*L*, II, 469–70)

Everything in the spring is indeed alive, including the wagons buried to their "stomachs" in mud. The playful comment that "Noah would have liked mother" returning from the outside with a burdock on her shawl to prove the snows have receded springs from a mind in good humor—one capable of experiencing great joy and love for all persons and things around her.

Her letters, however, have also dealt with death and with great sadness. Her nephew, Gilbert, had been a healthy and happy child; and his presence had a wholesome and unifying influence on all the Dickinsons. His parents, Austin and Sue, who had been drifting apart for years, were somewhat reconciled through their mutual love for the boy. The sisters, Emily and Lavinia, who had been finding it increasingly difficult to maintain cordial relations with their sister-in-law also came to a settlement of differences through Gilbert. His sudden death, then, from typhoid fever at the age of eight years was a great blow to the whole family. Even Emily, who had not entered her brother's house for fifteen years, did so on the night of Gilbert's death. Her elegaic letter to Sue after the boy died is one of her most powerful and beautiful letters, which in a mystical way emphasizes life and the triumph of immortality:

The Vision of Immortal Life has been fulfilled—

How simply at the last the Fathom comes! The Passenger and not the Sea, we find surprises us—

Gilbert rejoiced in Secrets—

His Life was panting with them—With what menace of Light he cried "Don't tell, Aunt Emily"! Now my ascended Playmate must instruct *me*. Show us, prattling Preceptor, but the way to thee!

He knew no niggard moment—His life was full of Boon—The Playthings of the Dervish were not so wild as his—

No crescent was this Creature—He traveled from the Full—

Such soar, but never set—
I see him in the Star, and meet his sweet velocity in everything that flies—His Life was like the Bugle, which winds itself away, his Elegy an echo—his Requiem ecstasy—
Dawn and Meridian in one.
Wherefore would he wait, wronged only of Night, which he left for us—
Without a speculation, our little Ajax spans the whole—

> Pass to thy Rendezvous of Light,
> Pangless except for us—
> Who slowly ford the Mystery
> Which thou hast leaped across!

(*L*, III, 799)

This moving letter contains nearly a perfect blending of prose and poetry. From the opening two lines, the poetic element is present in the imagery. The rhythm of the prose becomes gradually more metrical until the middle of the letter where there are six lines each with three beats: "He knew no niggard moment—/ His Life was full of Boon—/The Playthings of the Dervish/were not so wild as his—/No crescent was this Creature—/He traveled from the Full—." Prose then returns only to end in a straightforward stanza which crystallizes the poet's sense of the mystery of death.

III *The Higginson Correspondence*

There is a surprising number of notable persons among Dickinson's nearly one hundred known correspondents. For example, the Reverend Charles Wadsworth was a widely praised pulpit orator considered second only to Henry Ward Beecher; Samuels Bowles was the renowned editor of the nationally reputed *Springfield Republican;* Helen Hunt Jackson was a bestselling poet and novelist; Josiah G. Holland, also a bestselling novelist, was the editor of *Scribner's Monthly Magazine;* and Judge Otis P. Lord was a distinguished member of the Massachusetts Supreme Court. Many others with whom she corresponded, while not themselves New England luminaries, were, however, usually close to those who were. A few examples of this category are Maria Whitney, sister of a famous philologist and geologist for whom California's Mount Whitney was named; Franklin B. Sanborn, biographer of Thoreau; Mrs. Lucius Boltwood, cousin to Emerson; Mabel Loomis Todd, a correspondent with William Dean Howells and with the Thoreau family; Emily Fowler, granddaughter of Noah Webster; and Frances and Louise Norcross, friends of the sculptor, Daniel Chester French.

On April 15, 1862, Emily Dickinson added another name to her list of important correspondents with the following letter:

> Mr. Higginson,
> Are you too deeply occupied to say if my Verse is alive?
> The Mind is so near itself—it cannot see, distinctly—and I have none to ask—
> Should you think it breathed—and had you the leisure to tell me, I should feel quick gratitude—
> If I make the mistake—that you dared to tell me—would give me sincerer honor—toward you—
> I enclose my name—asking you, if you please—Sir—to tell me what is true?
> That you will not betray me—it is needless to ask—since Honor is it's own pawn—(*L*, II, 403)

At the time this letter was written, Thomas Wentworth Higginson was a well-known and prolific writer, a leading spokesman of liberal New England social reform and a cultivated literary conservatism. A direct descendant of Bay Colony forebears whose name had been associated with Harvard College since its founding, he himself had graduated from Harvard's Divinity School and had been a pastor of a Unitarian Church in Newburyport from 1847 to 1849 and of a "Free Church" in Worcester from 1852 to 1861. But his outspoken social and political reform efforts and his active role in antislavery ventures took him so much farther and farther away from church duties that he withdrew altogether in 1861 from the clerical life to devote himself entirely to writing and to lecturing about social progress and literary criticism.

Higginson was not a great literary critic; he was merely a representative one of mid-nineteenth-century America. He was subject to the same values, ambitions, and prejudices of the average lot. He lacked the luster of a Bryant or Lowell and the genius of an Emerson. His response, for instance, to Walt Whitman's masterpiece was typical: "It is no discredit to Walt Whitman that he wrote 'Leaves of Grass,' only that he did not burn it afterwards."[9] If he had not attracted something in Emily Dickinson which caused her to begin a lifelong correspondence with him, he might not now have very much literary immortality.

Dickinson's first letter to Higginson, quoted above, was written after reading his "Letter to a Young Contributor," the lead article in the *Atlantic Monthly* for April, 1862.[10] His essay was addressed to all would-be writers and is full of practical advice about manuscript preparation, as well as encouragement and suggestions regarding taste and style that emphasize verbal smoothness and the avoidance of wordiness and obtuse language. In his essay he wrote "Charge your style with life"; and Dickinson asked, in her letter to him, if her verse was "alive" and if it "breathed." She came to him as an unknown poet seeking the advice of a then famous critic, and the tenseness she felt is reflected somewhat in her taut prose. But she did not come to him overly humble as such slightly ironic phrases as "are you too deeply occupied," "had you the leisure to tell me," and "that you dared to tell me" seem to suggest. Besides, she enclosed four poems with this letter that violated nearly all the rules he suggested for poetry—"Safe in their Alabaster Chambers," "The nearest Dream recedes unrealized," "We play at Paste," and "I'll tell you how the Sun rose." Only the last one approaches either the conventional and or what might have been familiar in the way of poetry to Higginson. All four, however, are characterized by typical Dickinsonian irregularities—off-rhymes, mixed meters, unusual syntax, and the use of dashes for punctuation. So, it would appear, she was not out to ensnare his approval.

Unfortunately, almost all of his correspondence to her is lost, so we do not know exactly how he replied, although we can reconstruct it somewhat from her next letter to him. Besides commenting on her poems with apparently some recommendations for changing them or regularizing them (she called it "surgery"), he asked her age; something about her friends, family, and reading interests; and if she were perhaps influenced by either Whitman or Harriet Prescott Spofford, if she were interested in publishing, and finally, perhaps, why she had chosen to write to him. Her second letter to him is somewhat more expansive, but it is reserved enough to leave some questions about her still unanswered:

> Thank you for the surgery—it was not so painful as I supposed. I bring you others—as you ask—though they might not differ—. . .
>
> You asked how old I was? I made no verse—but one or two—until this winter—Sir—
>
> I had a terror—since September—I could tell to none—and so I sing, as the Boy does by the Burying Ground—because I am afraid—You inquire my Books—For Poets—I have Keats—and Mr and Mrs Browning. For Prose—Mr Ruskin—Sir Thomas Browne—and the Revelations. I went to

school—but in your manner of the phrase—had no education. When a little Girl, I had a friend, who taught me Immortality—but venturing too near, himself—he never returned—Soon after, my Tutor, died—and for several years, my Lexicon—was my only companion—Then I found one more—but he was not contented I be his scholar—so he left the Land.

You ask of my Companions Hills—Sir—and the Sundown—and a Dog—large as myself, That my Father bought me—They are better than Beings—because they know—but do not tell—and the noise in the Pool, at Noon—excels my Piano. I have a Brother and Sister—My Mother does not care for thought—and Father, too busy with his Briefs—to notice what we do—He buys me many Books—But begs me not to read them—because he fears they joggle the Mind. They are religious—except me—and address and Eclipse, every morning—whom they call their "Father." But I fear my story fatigues you—I would like to learn—could you tell me how to grow—or is it unconveyed—like Melody—or Witchcraft?

You speak of Mr. Whitman—I never read his Book—but was told that he was disgraceful—

I read Miss Prescott's "Circumstance," but it followed me, in the Dark—so I avoided her—

Two Editors of Journals came to my Father's House, this winter—and asked me for my Mind—and when I asked them "Why," they said I was Penurious—and they, would use it for the World—

I could not weigh myself—Myself—

My size felt small—to me—I read your Chapters in the Atlantic—and experienced honor for you—I was sure you would not reject a confiding question—

Is this—Sir—what you asked me to tell you? (*L*, II, 404–5)

Although she thanked him for his advice, she was apparently not going to follow it; for she admits at the start that she has enclosed other poems of the same kind. With this letter, she sent "There came a Day at Summer's full," "Of all the Sounds despatched abroad," and "South Winds jostle them." She evaded the question of her age, and she conceals the fact that by this time she had written some three hundred poems.

The "terror—since September" has caused scholars endless trouble. Since it has usually been thought to refer to the loss of a secret lover, the identity of the lover has fascinated scholars; and they have searched column upon column of obituaries trying to find him. However, Ruth Miller's estimate of the phrase's meaning seems most rational at this point. Since it is linked with the phrase "I sing, as the Boy does by the Burying Ground—because I am afraid" may refer the "terror" simply to her continued fear of death which the writing of poetry helps to relieve.[11] As to her comments about her friends and her family, the friend who taught her immortality was Benjamin Newton (1821–1853), with whom as a young girl she talked of poetry and of her own verse. After this "Tutor" died, she found one more who "left the Land." Reverend Charles Wadsworth, Major Hunt, and George Gould have all been suggested as the man; but recent scholarship would uphold the name of Samuel Bowles who had sailed for Europe only a few weeks before this letter was written. The description of her parents is mildly critical, but her evaluation of the family's religion is seriously so. She almost equates their faith with a mindlessly primitive worship of the sun. The two editors she refers to are Samuel Bowles and Dr. Holland, but their wanting her "Mind . . . for the world" is clearly overstated.

Although a good deal of honest information about herself emerges from this letter, however cryptically it is told, there is also a good deal of posing. She was much more accomplished as a poet than she was letting be known, and she also had a great deal more insight and self-confidence regarding her craft than the letter reveals. Finally, the little girl's voice at the end of the letter appears merely ingratiating.

Higginson's second letter had apparently praised her poems, for her third letter to him opens effusively: "Your letter gave no Drunkenness, because I tasted Rum before—Domingo comes but once—yet I have had few pleasures so deep as your opinion, and if I tried to thank you, my tears would block my tongue—" (*L*, II, 408). As grateful as she was for his praise, she was still unwilling to accept his advice and write by the conventional rules of prosody. He had apparently suggested she either regularize her meters and rhymes or drop them altogether to write free verse. Her reply is friendly but firm:

> Your second letter surprised me, and for a moment, swung—I had not supposed it. Your first—gave no dishonor, because the True—are not ashamed—I thanked you for your justice—but could not drop the Bells whose jingling cooled my Tramp—Perhaps the Balm, seemed better, because you bled me, first. . . .
>
> You think my gait "spasmodic"—I am in danger—Sir—
>
> You think me "uncontrolled"—I have no Tribunal. *L*, II, 408–9)

Her comments are important because they establish her convictions about her art and her determination to follow them at whatever cost. She makes an existential decision to keep the music of her verse, her jingling bells, no matter if her poetry is "spasmodic" and "uncontrolled." If this decision to write by her own standards meant sacrificing the chance to be published and to achieve recognition as a poet, she accepted it nonetheless. With courage and a wise faith in herself, she also writes:

> I smile when you suggest that I delay "to publish"—that being foreign to my thought, as Firmament to Fin—
>
> If fame belonged to me, I could not escape her—if she did not, the longest day would pass me on the chase—and the approbation of my Dog, would forsake me—then—My Barefoot—Rank is better—. (*L*, II, 408)

Aware of the differences of opinion which separated her from Higginson, she set down the rules by which they would correspond: "If I might bring you what I do—not so frequent to trouble you—and ask you if I told it clear—'twould be control, to me—" (*L*, II, 409). She would send him poetry from time to time, and he would tell her if it was "clear," but she does not promise to follow his recommendations. She obviously needed his friendship; and, even though he lacked discernment as to her purpose as an artist, she needed to feel, as all poets have, that she had access to a respectable audience, however narrow.

In her fourth letter, despite the fact that she had already abandoned her need for his recommendations, she pleaded that he give them to her: "Will you tell me my fault, frankly as to yourself, for I had rather wince, than die. Men do not call the surgeon, to commend—the Bone, but to set it, Sir, and fracture within, is more critical. And for this, Preceptor, I shall bring you—Obedience—the Blossom from my Garden, and every gratitude I know" (*L*, II, 412). It is indeed possible that she is again trying to ingratiate herself, for she sounds very much like a little naughty girl who is always promising to do better although she has neither the will nor any real desire to improve. The interpretation seems valid, for she enclosed within this letter four poems which were bound to violate once again Higginson's sense of what poetry ought to be. With this letter she sent "Of Tribulation these are they," "Your Riches taught me poverty," "Some keep the Sabbath going to Church," and "Success is counted sweetest"; and none of these poems is any more conventional than the previous poems she had sent. Nonetheless, she signed this letter "Your Scholar," a practice that was also used in later letters to him.

Dickinson's correspondence with Higginson begins at this point to look like something of a charade. She would play the inquiring scholar asking for the instructions she had no intention of using, and he was to play the pretended preceptor who presented the lessons that would not be learned. She wanted this formality imposed upon their friendship; and Higginson, because of respect for her or because of confusion, was apparently willing to cooperate. Since every game has its rules, she clarified hers: "Because you have much business, beside the growth of me—you will appoint, yourself, how often I shall come—without your inconvenience. And if at any time—you regret you received me, or I prove a different fabric to that you supposed—you must banish me—" (*L*, II, 412).

That Higginson was immediately or later aware of the game and its rules and that he was willing to cooperate is evident from an essay about their correspondence that he wrote years later for the *Atlantic Monthly*: ". . . we corresponded at varying intervals, she always persistently keeping up this attitude of 'Scholar,' and assuming on my part of preceptorship which it is almost needless to say did not exist. Always glad to hear her 'recite,' as she called it, I soon abandoned all attempt to guide in the slightest degree this extraordinary nature, and simply accepted her confidences, giving as much as I could of what might interest her in return."[12] Later in the essay he again acknowledges that her need for his interest lay outside her wish for his criticism: ". . . on my side an interest that was strong and even affectionate, but not based on any thorough comprehension; and on her side a hope, always rather baffled, that I should afford some aid in solving her abstruse problem of life."[13]

Although scholars have been tempted to ridicule Higginson for his conservatism and for his misunderstanding of Dickinson's poetic craft, he is to be credited, in the final analysis, for accepting his role in the correspondence and for continuing to respond to her as a friend who offered encouragement and support. The function he fulfilled, one somewhat hidden from our understanding, was of the utmost importance to Emily Dickinson; for she acknowledged in a letter to him six years later her great debt of gratitude: "Of our greatest acts we are ignorant—You were not aware that you saved my Life. To thank you in person has been since then one of my few requests" (*L*, II, 460). Whether he actually or symbolically "saved her life," she indeed meant her statement seriously; for, eleven years later, in another letter, she again refers to him as "the Friend that saved my Life" (*L*, II, 649).

Dickinson's correspondence with Higginson continued for the rest of her life; for, though occasionally only a letter a year was exchanged when other interests or responsibilities intervened for both, they always resumed their writing to each other with more frequency. She continued to send him poems, to ask for his advice, and to maintain the fiction that she was his pupil. Eventually, their correspondence widened to include subjects of personal importance; and each correspondent's deep regard for the well-being and happiness of the other pervades the later letters as do heartfelt statements of condolence or congratulation when losses or changes occurred.

Higginson visited Emily Dickinson twice during her lifetime, and his impressions of her are the best record we have of her appearance and manners. In a letter to his wife after his first visit, he described Dickinson:

> A step like a pattering child's in entry & in glided a little plain woman with two smooth bands of reddish hair . . . in a very plain & exquisitely clean white pique & a blue net worsted shawl. She came to me with two day lilies, which she put in a sort of childlike way into my hand & said, "These are my introduction" in a soft frightened breathless childlike voice—and added under her breath, Forgive me if I am frightened; I never see strangers and hardly know what to say—but she talked soon & thenceforward continuously—& deferentially—sometimes stopping to ask me to talk instead of her—but readily recommencing. . . . thoroughly ingenuous & simple . . . & saying many things which you would have thought foolish & I wise—& some things you wd. hv. liked.[14]

He then wrote some twenty of her aphoristic comments in her words, as well as his as best as he could remember them. "If I read a book & it makes my whole body so cold no fire ever can warm me I know *that* is poetry. If I feel physically as if the top of my head were taken off, I know *that* is poetry." "Truth is such a *rare* thing, it is delightful to tell it." "I find ecstasy in living—the mere sense of living is joy enough."[15] Twenty years later Higginson recalled that not a trace of affectation existed in her manner or in her speech, but he concluded that still she eluded him: "She was much too enigmatical a being for me to solve in an hour's interview, and an instinct told me that the slightest attempt at direct cross-examination would make her withdraw into her shell; I could only sit still and watch, as one does in the woods; I must name my bird without a gun, as recommended by Emerson."[16]

During the quarter of a century that they corresponded, Higginson had received a hundred poems from Dickinson; and, shortly after her death, he agreed to edit with Mabel Loomis Todd the first volumes of Dickinson's *Poems* that appeared in 1890 and 1891. However, he did so reluctantly because he had never become fully convinced that publishing them was a sound critical decision or assessment. Right to the end, Dickinson's soul and art eluded him. What he wrote of her after years of knowing her and her poetry capsulizes the perplexity of a lifetime spent with a personality and genius beyond his ability to comprehend: "The impression of a wholly new and original poetic genius was as distinct on my mind . . . as it is now, after thirty years of further knowledge; and with it came the problem never yet solved, what place ought to be assigned in literature to what is so remarkable, yet so elusive of criticism. The bee himself did not evade the schoolboy more than she evaded me; and even at this day I still stand somewhat bewildered, like the boy."[17]

CHAPTER 8

A Lasting Influence

EMILY Dickinson's poetry is so nearly unique and its publication to the world so irregular that it is difficult to trace her influence upon particular later writers. For years after the first appearance of her poetry in the selected version *Poems by Emily Dickinson*, edited by Mabel Loomis Todd and T. W. Higginson in 1890, her poems continued to be issued in piecemeal fashion and usually in awkwardly edited versions. It was not until sixty-five years later that a definitive edition of all her poems in their original forms was published under the skillful editorship of Thomas H. Johnson. Nevertheless, their durability—their modernity or, perhaps, their eternality—has proven sufficient to sustain them; and they have been admired by a vast number of widely diverse twentieth-century artists.

The mere list of the poets and the poet-critics who have written poetic tributes to her and essays about her work would fill a sizeable page. Among those who have praised and championed her work, or acknowledged Dickinson's deep impression upon them are Conrad Aiken, Louise Bogan, John Ciardi, Gregory Corso, Hart Crane, J. V. Cunningham, Amy Lowell, Archibald MacLeish, Ron Padgett, John Crowe Ransom, Adrienne Rich, Carl Sandburg, Karl Shapiro, Allen Tate, Mark Van Doren, Richard Wilbur, and Yvor Winters. As the range and the diversity of this list implies, Emily Dickinson has appealed to poets of all persuasions from every decade of this century. In fact, her influence has extended to other arts besides the literary, since renowned composers such as Aaron Copland and Ned Rorem have set her poems to music and since Martha Graham, the great modern dancer, choreographed a performance based on the poet's life.

The poems written by other poets in tribute to Dickinson are somewhat hard to judge, since they straddle a borderline between emotional attachment and rational criticism. What emerges from most of them is a sense of the spontaneous appreciation one craftsman may feel for another. Hart Crane, whose major poetic achievement was *The Bridge* (1930), pays homage to Dickinson in a poem about her poetic vision and life of suffering:

> O sweet, dead Silencer, most suddenly clear
> When singing that Eternity possessed
> And plundered momently in every breast;
>
> —Truly no flower yet withers in your hand,
> The harvest you described and understand
> Needs more than wit to gather, love to bind.[1]

After an uncomfortable complaint about Emily's sheltered life, Gregory Corso, a "Beat" poet who rose out of the 1950s, concludes his poem to her by affirming how reading her poetry has altered his perceptions:

> Good lady I love you
> I can't look at a fly with my obvious betterness
> And ask Why.[2]

Adrienne Rich's poem "E." is a sympathetic attempt to reach an understanding of the real poet behind the confusing and sometimes contradictory versions of her that scholars have created. Beginning with ironic comments about academics and antiquarians who have tried to preserve and "monumentalize" the poet, Rich acknowledges Dickinson's dedication to "the word" and the necessity of her withdrawal:

> you, woman, masculine
> in singlemindedness
> for whom the word was more
> than a symptom—
>
> a condition of being.
> Till the air buzzing with spoiled language
> sang in your ears
> of Perjury

and in your halfcracked way you chose
silence for entertainment,
chose to have it out at last
on your own premises.[3]

I *Imagism*

One of the earliest poet-critics to acknowledge Dickinson's influence was the Imagist, Amy Lowell. In her poems and essays, she paid tribute to Dickinson as "one of the greatest women poets who ever lived,"[4] and she recognized her as a predecessor of modern poetry and as a forerunner of imagism. In a lecture that Lowell gave in Boston in 1915 that was entitled "The New Manner in Modern Poetry," she rejected most of nineteenth-century American poetry as imitative and derivative, with the exceptions of the unappreciated genuises, Poe and Whitman. At the end of the Civil War, "poetry alone was inert. Inert, that is, save for one still, small voice. One little voice which was the precursor of the modern day. A voice considered only as bizarre and not at all important, by its contemporaries. I refer to Emily Dickinson, who is so modern that if she were living today I know just the group of poets with whom she would inevitably belong."[5] The group Lowell refers to, of course, was comprised of Imagists.

In another lecture less than a year later in Connecticut on "American Poets of Today," Lowell again denounced nineteenth-century poetry except for Poe, Whitman, and Dickinson. In this lecture-essay, she presented more detail about Dickinson's background and temperament; and she described her as a latter-day revolutionary:

> Strangely enough, there started up in New England a rare (if it had not really existed I should have said an "impossible") anomaly. A true pagan poet shut up in the cage of a narrow provincial Puritanism. But the odd part of this poet was that the cage was not merely the exterior one of family and surroundings, it was the cage of her own soul. I refer, of course, to Emily Dickinson. She was a pagan if ever there was one, but she was also a sincerely religious woman. This led her to address poems to the Deity in so joyous and familiar a strain that her first biographer wrote many pages to explain her seeming irreverence. . . . I have often wondered whether this duality of temperament was not responsible for the shyness and elusive quality which she is said to have had in a marked degree. In wider sur-

roundings might she not have developed into a greater poet and a more tranquil woman?[6]

Lowell's rejection of nineteenth-century poetry, with the exception of the triad of poets, recurs a third time in her long poem, *A Critical Fable*. In the framework of a debate between James Russell Lowell, her famous ancestor, and an unnamed persona, Amy Lowell upholds Dickinson as one of the few poets she sincerely admires:

"Your strange estimation has made me quite jealous
For those of my time whose secure reputations
Gave us no concern. These are trifling vexations,
But they itch my esteem. Is there really not one
You sincerely admire?" "Yes, Miss Dickinson,"
I hastily answered. At this he stopped dead
In his walk and his eyes seemed to pop from his head.
"What," he thundered, "that prim and perverse
little person
Without an idea you could hang up a verse on!
Wentworth Higginson did what he could, his tuition
Was ardent, unwearied, but bore no fruition."[7]

In 1918, Lowell delivered two lectures at the Brooklyn Institute on "Imagism Past and Present"; and in this lecture-essay she traced the roots of the movement that she, Ezra Pound, Hilda Doolittle, and John Gould Fletcher, among others, worked to establish. Imagism was a revolt against imprecision and sentimentality in poetry, and its proponents strove for the clear, concentrated poetic image; for the free choice of any subject; for expression in common speech free of cliché and with new appropriate rhythms. In her lectures, she traced imagism from Theocritus to William Blake, to Samuel Taylor Coleridge, and to Emily Dickinson—all of whom had revitalized poetry at the end of some literary era. She evaluated Dickinson as a forerunner of imagism because of her usage, her experimentation with meter and rhyme, and her "unrelated method" of writing—"That is, the describing of a thing by its appearance only without regard to its entity in any other way."[8] As an example, Lowell quoted "A route of evanescence."

When Amy Lowell died suddenly in 1925, she left unwritten the biography of Emily Dickinson that she had always wished to do. Her last discussion of Dickinson occurs in the first posthumous volume of her poetry, *What's O'Clock*. In the poem, "The Sisters", she assembles a trio of the poets she feels closest to—Sappho, Elizabeth Barrett Browning, and Emily Dickinson. She describes her love for Dickinson in an imaginary visit with the poet as she is contemplating a hummingbird in her garden:

> . . . Not having expected strangers,
> She might forget to think me one, and holding up
> A finger say quite casually: "Take care
> Don't frighten him, he's only just begun."
> "Now this," I well believe I should have thought,
> "Is even better than Sapho. With Emily
> You're really here, or never anywhere at all
> In range of mind." Wherefore, having begun
> In the strict centre, we could slowly progress
> To various circumferences, as we pleased.
> We could, but should we? That would quite depend
> On Emily. I think she'd be exacting,
> Without intention possibly, and ask
> A thousand tight-rope tricks of understanding.
> But, bless you, I would somersault all day
> If by doing I might stay with her.
> I hardly think that we should mention souls
> Although they might just round the corner from us
> In some half-quizzical, half-wistful metaphor.
> I'm very sure that I should never seek
> To turn her parables to stated fact.[9]

The poem ends with a farewell to the three poets and with the observation, "I understand you all, for in myself—/Is that presumption? Yet indeed it's true—/We are one family."[10]

II *Three Views*

Among our contemporary poet-critics who have written about the influence of Dickinson are Archibald MacLeish, Louise Bogan, and Richard Wilbur; and their essays at the bicentennial celebration of the town of Amherst in 1959, appear in a slender, though important volume entitled *Emily Dickinson: Three Views.*[11] MacLeish focuses on the voice of the poet which, he says, supplies the key to her work; Bogan considers Dickinson in the tradition of mystical poetry; and Wilbur discusses her poetic technique and state of mind. Speaking from the point of view of fellow craftsmen, each poet relates Dickinson to the modern reader.

MacLeish calls Dickinson "one of the most important of modern poets," and he describes the tone of voice in the poems as typically modern. He characterizes her poetic voice as "spontaneous," "dramatic," urgent, and immediate. She learned "a curiously compounded colloquialism . . . almost a century before" Ezra Pound turned to it for his translation of *The Women of Trachis*. MacLeish affirms "that without her extraordinary mastery of tone her achievement would have been impossible."[12]

Bogan finds a universality and timelessness in Dickinson's mystical poetry as she looks backward to Dante and St. John of the Cross and forward to William Butler Yeats and T. S. Eliot. Yet, Bogan maintains, "At the highest summit of her art, she resembles no one. She begins to cast toward the future: to produce poems in which we recognize, as one French critic has said, both the *voyant* faculty of Rimbaud and Mallarmé's feeling for the mystery and sacredness of the word."[13]

Wilbur discovers in Dickinson a set of values and attitudes that we have come to associate with the strictly modern poets who are living in a science-dominated world that is impressed with the theories of Sigmund Freud and Albert Einstein. He writes that her poems "appeal to experience," for they are motivated by a "passion for the truth," "objective fact," "accuracy," and solid detail. Like poets under the influence of modern psychology, "her chief truthfulness lay in her insistence on discovering the facts of her inner experience. She was a Linnaeus to the phenomena of her own consciousness, describing and distinguishing the states and motions of her soul." Writing about her own mind with such penetration was her innovation to the art of poetry. She took poetry to a region "which poetry had never so sharply defined." What Dickinson discovered about the world and her own soul, Wilbur equates with the philosophical notions of the modern existentialist: "that the aspect of the world is in no way constant, that the power of external things depends on our state of mind, that the soul selects its own society and may, if granted strength to do so, select a superior order and scope of consciousness which will render it finally invulnerable."[14]

III *Modernity*

A number of techniques and stylistic innovations in Dickinson's poetry anticipated the concerns of modern poets. Although it is impossible to judge whether or not her practice directly influenced theirs, it is certain that her striking aesthetic effects account for a good deal of the attention given her by twentieth-century writers. Scholars have enjoyed placing her, therefore, within a tradition leading to modern poetry. Albert J. Gelpi's view is a widely accepted one:

> When it came to specific matters of approach and technique, when it came to writing a poem and practicing her craft, she did not belong to the prophetic or Dionysian strain of American poetry which derived palely from Emerson and descended lustily through Whitman to Carl Sandburg and Jeffers, . . . the deliberate and formalistic quality of Dickinson's verse associates her rather with the diverse yet Apollonian tradition which proceeds from Edward Taylor through her to Eliot, Stevens, Frost, and Marianne Moore, and thence to Robert Lowell and Elizabeth Bishop.[15]

A good indication of her connection to these modern poets is her "insatiable and unabating interest in the wiles of words." Enumerating the aspects of her verbal magic, Gelpi writes:

> She chose words with stinging freshness; she flavored speech with earthy New England colloquialisms; she often dropped the "s" of the third-person of the present tense to suggest the enduring quality of the action; she emphasized nouns by the striking addition or omission of the preceding article; she sometimes used singular nouns where plurals were expected and vice versa; she made parts of speech perform unorthodox functions, used words in startling contexts, coined words when none seemed available or apt. Like Ezra Pound, William Carlos Williams, Marianne Moore, and E. E. Cummings, Emily Dickinson sought to speak the uniqueness of her experience in a personal tongue by reconstituting and revitalizing—at the risk of eccentricity—the basic verbal unit.[16]

In addition, as Brita Lindberg-Seyersted has noted about Dickinson's language, the frequent use of scientific words and technical terminology (for example, "atom," "circumference," "contusion," "hermetic," "iodine," and "perihelion") look toward the modern poet.[17]

Not only is Emily Dickinson's language modern, but her rhymes and use of imagery have also been noted as uniquely contemporary. Brita Lindberg-Seyersted, after discussing the several categories of near rhymes in Dickinson's verse, concludes that "no poet writing before the last quarter of the nineteenth century seems to have employed these types of rhyme as frequently and as deliberately as Dickinson." This uniqueness in her style, she asserts, "places her among the moderns, who demand less identity among sounds—in poetry as in music—to satisfy and please the ear than had been prescribed by an earlier taste."[18] Among the modern poets representing this aspect of Dickinson's modernity, Lindberb-Seyersted names Gerard Manley Hopkins, Yeats, Wilfred Owen, and W. H. Auden.

In a brief article, "Emily Dickinson and Twentieth-Century Poetry of Sensibility," Suzanne M. Wilson notes the complex technique in Dickinson's use of imagery that has become important in contemporary poetry. Although Dickinson used the rigid, rational, sermonic structure for much of her poetry, she frequently employed images which depended for their full comprehension upon the reader's intuition and his awareness of numerous associations suggested by the image. Wilson compares Dickinson's technique with that of Pound, Eliot, and the American Imagists. "It is in her use of suggestion, both free and limited," she writes, "as well as in her use of sharp, extended images that Emily Dickinson most resembles twentieth-century poets who developed their techniques after the pattern of the French Symbolists and Japanese poets."[19]

IV *Conclusion*

How may we account for these similarities and analogies between Emily Dickinson and contemporary poets? Why is it that she seems to hold a unique claim upon the mind of modern man, and that what she speaks to us appears fresh and relevant despite the years and changes which separate us from her? In answer to such questions, we recognize that her rigorous intellectuality, her appreciation for definition, and her sense of the inevitability of fact recommends her to an age dominated by science. She scorns the pedantry of the classifiers, but her numerous nature poems, as well as those poems which explore her emotional and psychological states, are characterized by sharp, accurate detail, the result of careful research and scientific observation.

In addition, her sense of the anguish of personal existence and of the fragility of all life that appears in her greatest lyrics about death and immortality reflects our own helpless state of mind when we witness the torturous social evils which plague our world and an environment which appears to be progressively worsening. We also see in her finest poems the same paradoxical mixture of desire and reluctance, of will and withdrawal, of hope and fear which characterize our own efforts at living a fully human life. Like her, we are looking for God yet doubting that he will be good; we want to live in harmony with nature but are terrified by the vast indifference of an infinite universe; we want love, but we live defensively in isolation within our overcrowded cities.

Truly, modern man may learn a great deal from the example of Dickinson. In our era, which has made death an institution and which has taught itself the multifarious forms of lethal behavior, courage and the will to endure are virtues that come immediately to mind from a reading of Emily Dickinson. The need for commitment and the necessary exclusions and self-denials which the mind must make to preserve its identity and its stability also come through Dickinson to an age bombarded with trivia, distraction, and mediocrity. Finally, that the human spirit may be rejuvenated, amended, and healed by the perception and application of truth and beauty is perhaps the most important legacy Emily Dickinson has bequeathed to a restless and troubled modern age.

Notes and References

Chapter One

1. Martha Dickinson Bianchi, *The Single Hound* (Boston, 1914), p. xviii.
2. Martha Dickinson Bianchi, *The Life and Letters of Emily Dickinson* (Boston, 1924), pp. 43–51.
3. Josephine Pollitt, *Emily Dickinson: The Human Background of Her Poetry* (New York, 1930), pp. 119–56.
4. Genevieve Taggard, *The Life and Mind of Emily Dickinson* (New York, 1920), pp. 91ff.
5. MacGregor Jenkins, *Emily Dickinson, Friend and Neighbor* (Boston, 1930).
6. Susan Glaspell, *Alison's House: A Play in Three Acts* (New York, 1930), p. 25.
7. Ibid., p. 139.
8. Ibid., p. 5.
9. In *The Burns Mantle Best Plays of 1947–48*, ed. John Chapman (New York, 1948), p. 247.
10. Ibid., p. 261.
11. Ibid., p. 258.
12. George Frisbie Whicher, *This Was a Poet: A Critical Biography of Emily Dickinson* (New York 1939), p. 101.
13. Norman Rosten, *Come Slowly Eden* (New York, 1967), p. 10.
14. Ibid., p. 14.
15. Macgregor Jenkins, *Emily* (Indianapolis, 1930), p. 7.
16. Laura Benet, *Come Slowly Eden* (New York, 1942), p. ix.
17. Ibid., pp. 263–64.
18. Whicher, pp. 20–21.
19. Jay Leyda, *The Years and Hours of Emily Dickinson* (New Haven, 1960), I, 4.
20. Whicher, p. 27.
21. *The Letters of Emily Dickinson*, ed. Thomas H. Johnson and Theodora Ward (Cambridge, Mass., 1958), II, 528. All selections from the letters

of Emily Dickinson are drawn from this edition, and will be indicated in the text by the capital letter *L*, followed by the volume and pages of the reference, enclosed in parentheses as in (*L*, II, 528).

22. Leyda, II, 152.

23. See affectionate references to her mother in *L*, III, 746, 754, and 771.

24. Quoted in Whicher, p. 34.

Chapter Two

1. Allen Tate, "Emily Dickinson," in *Emily Dickinson: A Collection of Critical Essays*, ed. Richard B. Sewall (Englewood Cliffs, N.J., 1963), p. 27.

2. Ibid., pp. 16–27.

3. *The Poems of Emily Dickinson*, ed. Thomas H. Johnson (Cambridge, Mass., 1955), I, 270. All selections from the poems of Emily Dickinson are drawn from this edition, and will be indicated in the text by the capital letter *P*, followed by the poem number, then the volume and pages of the reference, enclosed in parentheses as in (*P*, 338; I, 270).

4. Henry W. Wells, *Introduction to Emily Dickinson* (Chicago, 1947), pp. 257–58.

5. Clark Griffith, *The Long Shadow: Emily Dickinson's Tragic Poetry* (Princeton, N.J., 1964), pp. 261–65.

6. Hyatt H. Waggoner, "Proud Ephemeral: Emily Dickinson," in *American Poets: From the Puritans to the Present* (Boston, 1968), pp. 181–222; Albert J. Gelpi, *Emily Dickinson: The Mind of the Poet* (Cambridge, Mass., 1965), passim.

7. Austin Warren, "Emily Dickinson," in *Emily Dickinson: A Collection of Critical Essays*, p. 106.

8. Charles R. Anderson, *Emily Dickinson's Poetry: Stairway of Surprise* (New York, 1960), p. 273.

Chapter Three

1. Millicent Todd Bingham, *Emily Dickinson's Home* (New York, 1955), pp. 179–80.

2. Griffith, p. 140.

3. John Cody, *After Great Pain: The Inner Life of Emily Dickinson* (Cambridge, Mass., 1971), p. 272.

4. See "Where bells no more affright the morn (*P*, 112; I, 82–83); "It's like the Light" (*P*, 297; I, 216–17); and "There is a Zone whose even Years (*P*, 1056; II, 745).

5. Caroline Hogue, "Dickinson's 'I heard a Fly buzz—when I died'," *Explicator* 20 (November, 1961), item 26.

6. Griffith, p. 118.

7. Brita Lindberg-Seyersted, *The Voice of the Poet: Aspects of Style in the Poetry of Emily Dickinson* (Cambridge, Mass., 1968), p. 220.

8. Eunice Glenn, "Emily Dickinson's Poetry: A Revaluation," *The Sewanee Review* 51 (Autumn, 1943), 585.

9. Anderson, *Emily Dickinson's Poetry: Stairway of Surprise*, p. 243.

Chapter Four

1. The dates these poems appeared in the *Springfield Republican* are, in order of publication, February 20, 1852; March 1, 1862; May 4, 1862; March 30, 1864; and February 14, 1866.

2. Ruth Miller's discussion of the letters is covered in two chapters, "The Master Letters I: The Subject Matter," and "The Master Letters II: The Mask of Style," in *The Poetry of Emily Dickinson* (Middletown, Connecticut, 1968), pp. 144–88.

3. Ibid., p. 144.

4. For landmark analyses of this poem see, Clark Griffith, *The Long Shadow*, pp. 177–83; John B. Pickard, *Emily Dickinson: An Introduction and Interpretation* (New York, 1967), pp. 84–85; and John Cody, *After Great Pain*, pp. 180–82.

Chapter Five

1. Anna Mary Wells, "Was Emily Dickinson Psychotic?", *American Imago* 19 (Winter, 1962), 320.

2. Bingham, *Emily Dickinson's Home*, p. xv.

3. Thomas H. Johnson, *Emily Dickinson: An Interpretive Biography* (Cambridge, Mass., 1955), p. 51.

4. John Crowe Ransom, "Emily Dickinson: A Poet Restored," in *Emily Dickinson: A Collection of Critical Essays*, p. 100.

5. Theodora Ward, *The Capsule of the Mind: Chapters in the Life of Emily Dickinson* (Cambridge, Mass., 1961), p. 72.

6. Allen Tate, "Emily Dickinson," in *Emily Dickinson: A Collection of Critical Essays*, p. 20.

7. Anderson, *Emily Dickinson's Poetry: Stairway of Surprise*, pp. 294–95.

8. John Malcolm Brinnin, "Emily Dickinson, The Legend and the Poet" in *Emily Dickinson*, ed. John Malcolm Brinnin (New York, 1960), p. 13.

9. Griffith, p. 283.

10. David T. Porter, *The Art of Emily Dickinson's Early Poetry* (Cambridge, Mass., 1966), passim.

11. Lindberg-Seyersted, pp. 25–26.

12. Wells, pp. 29, 33, 37.

13. Ward, *The Capsule of the Mind*, p. 55.

14. William R. Sherwood, *Circumference and Circumstance: Stages in the Mind and Art of Emily Dickinson* (New York, 1968), pp. 138, 160.

15. Griffith, p. 207.

16. Cody, pp. 484–85.
17. Ward, *The Capsule of the Mind,* p. 60.
18. Anderson, *Emily Dickinson's Poetry: Stairway of Surprise,* pp. 211–13.
19. Pickard, p. 96.
20. Griffith, p. 191.
21. Johnson, *Emily Dickinson: An Interpretive Biography,* p. 212; Richard Chase, *Emily Dickinson* (New York, 1951), pp. 246–47.
22. Pickard, p. 104.
23. Sherwood, pp. 106–7; Anderson, *Emily Dickinson's Poetry: Stairway of Surprise,* pp. 208–9.
24. Griffith, p. 247.
25. Cody, p. 499.

Chapter Six

1. *Selections from Ralph Waldo Emerson: An Organic Anthology,* ed. Stephen Whicher (Boston, 1957), p. 24.
2. Jack L. Capps, *Emily Dickinson's Reading 1836–1886* (Cambridge, Mass., 1966), p. 117.
3. Anderson, *Emily Dickinson's Poetry: Stairway of Surprise,* p. 30.
4. Chase, p. 167.
5. Walt Whitman, "Song of Myself," in *Leaves of Grass and Selected Prose by Walt Whitman,* ed. John Kouwenhoven (New York, 1950), p. 75.
6. For a good, brief summation of the interpretations of this poem, see the selection of criticism on this poem in *14 by Emily Dickinson with Selected Criticism,* ed. Thomas M. Davis (Chicago and Atlanta, 1964), pp. 85–90. The critics summarized are Yvor Winters, Kate Flores, Laurence Perrine, and Eric W. Carlson.
7. Griffith, p. 22.
8. Anderson, *Emily Dickinson's Poetry: Stairway of Surprise,* p. 106.
9. Ibid., p. 152.

Chapter Seven

1. David Higgins, *Portrait of Emily Dickinson: The Poet and Her Prose* (New Brunswick, N.J., 1967), p. 6. Throughout this chapter I have relied on David Higgins's excellent scholarship as a source of information and insight.
2. Ibid., p. 7.
3. Chase, p. 259.
4. Milton Hindus, "Emily's Prose: A Note," *Kenyon Review* 2 (Winter, 1940), 90.
5. John Tyree Fain, " 'New Poems' of Emily Dickinson," *Modern Language Notes* 68 (February, 1953), 112–13.
6. Whicher, p. 144.
7. Higgins, p. 4.

8. Wells, *Introduction to Emily Dickinson*, p. 15.
9. Leyda, II, 127.
10. Thomas Wentworth Higginson, "Letter to a Young Contributor," *Atlantic Monthly* 9 (April, 1862), 401–11.
11. Miller, *The Poetry of Emily Dickinson*, pp. 69–70.
12. Thomas Wentworth Higginson, "Emily Dickinson's Letters," *Atlantic Monthly* 68 (October, 1891), 450.
13. Ibid., p. 453.
14. Leyda, II, 151.
15. Ibid.
16. Higginson, "Emily Dickinson's Letters," p. 453.
17. Ibid., p. 445.

Chapter Eight

1. Quoted in *The Recognition of Emily Dickinson: Selected Criticisms Since 1890*, ed. Caesar R. Blake and Carlton F. Wells (Ann Arbor, Mich., 1964), p. 130.
2. Gregory Corso, "Emily Dickenson [*sic*] The Trouble With You Is——," *Big Table* 1, no. 4 (1960), 87.
3. In Albert J. Gelpi, *Emily Dickinson: The Mind of the Poet*, p. xiii.
4. S. Foster Damon, *Amy Lowell: A Chronicle* (Boston, 1935), p. 611.
5. Ibid., p. 296
6. Ibid., pp. 331–32.
7. Amy Lowell, *A Critical Fable* (Boston, 1922), p. 7.
8. Amy Lowell, *Poetry and Poets: Essays*, (Boston, 1930), p. 107.
9. Amy Lowell, *What's O'Clock* (Boston, 1925), pp. 133–34.
10. Ibid., pp. 136–37.
11. Archibald MacLeish, "The Private World," Louise Bogan, "A Mystical Poet," and Richard Wilbur, "Sumptuous Destitution" in *Emily Dickinson: Three Views* (Amherst, Mass., 1960).
12. Archibald MacLeish, "The Private World," ibid., pp. 13, 23, 22.
13. Louise Bogan, "A Mystical Poetry," ibid., p. 32.
14. Richard Wilbur, "Sumptuous Destitution," ibid., pp. 35–36.
15. Gelpi, p. 146.
16. Ibid., p. 147
17. Lindberg-Seyersted, *The Voice of the Poet*, p. 75.
18. Ibid., p. 161.
19. Suzanne M. Wilson, "Emily Dickinson and Twentieth-Century Poetry of Sensibility," *American Literature* 36 (November, 1964), 354.

Selected Bibliography

PRIMARY SOURCES

1. Poetry (arranged chronologically)

Poems by Emily Dickinson. Edited by Mabel Loomis Todd and T. W. Higginson. Boston: Roberts Brothers, 1890.

Poems by Emily Dickinson, Second Series. Edited by T. W. Higginson and Mabel Loomis Todd. Boston: Roberts Brothers, 1891.

Poems by Emily Dickinson, Third Series. Edited by Mabel Loomis Todd. Boston: Roberts Brothers, 1896.

The Single Hound, Poems of a Lifetime by Emily Dickinson. Edited by Martha Dickinson Bianchi. Boston: Little Brown, 1914.

The Poems of Emily Dickinson. Edited by Martha Dickinson Bianchi and Alfred Leete Hampson. Boston: Little, Brown, 1937.

Bolts of Melody. New Poems of Emily Dickinson. Edited by Mabel Loomis Todd and Millicent Todd Bingham. New York: Harper, 1945.

The Poems of Emily Dickinson, Including Variant Readings Critically Compared With All Known Manuscripts. Edited by Thomas H. Johnson. 3 vols. Cambridge, Mass.: Harvard University Press, 1955.

The Complete Poems of Emily Dickinson. Edited by Thomas H. Johnson. Boston: Little, Brown, 1960.

Final Harvest: Emily Dickinson's Poems. Edited by Thomas H. Johnson. Boston: Little, Brown, 1962.

2. Letters (arranged chronologically)

Letters of Emily Dickinson. Edited by Mabel Loomis Todd. 2 vols. Boston: Roberts Brothers, 1894.

Letters of Emily Dickinson, New and Enlarged Edition. Edited by Mabel Loomis Todd. New York: Harper, 1931.

Emily Dickinson's Letters to Dr. and Mrs. Josiah Gilbert Holland. Edited by Theodora Van Wagener Ward. Cambridge, Mass.: Harvard University Press, 1951.

The Letters of Emily Dickinson. Edited by Thomas H. Johnson and Theodora Ward. 3 vols. Cambridge, Mass. Harvard University Press, 1958.

SECONDARY SOURCES

1. Bibliography and Concordance

ANON. *Emily Dickinson, December 10, 1830–May 15, 1886. A Bibliography.* Amherst, Mass.: Jones Library, 1930. Unannotated list of Dickinson editions and more than three hundred secondary items chronologically arranged. Includes George F. Whicher's centennial appraisal of Dickinson's achievement.

BUCKINGHAM, WILLIS J., ed. *Emily Dickinson: An Annotated Bibliography, Writings, Scholarship, Criticism, and Ana 1850–1968.* Bloomington: Indiana University Press, 1970. Most useful, complete bibliography to date of materials by and about Dickinson in English and foreign languages. Lists over twenty-six hundred items in eleven categories and includes an index of poetry explications.

CLENDENNING, SHEILA T. *Emily Dickinson: A Bibliography.* Kent, Ohio: Kent State University Press, 1968. Annotated listing of primary and secondary materials; omits short reviews and ana. Includes an introductory essay on the history of Dickinson scholarship.

FREIS, SUSAN. "Emily Dickinson: A Check List of Criticism, 1930–1966." *Papers of the Bibliographical Society of America* 61 (Fourth Quarter, 1967), 359–85. Limited annotation of some 465 items of scholarship. Especially useful for locating explications of Dickinson's poetry.

ROSENBAUM, S. P. *A Concordance to the Poems of Emily Dickinson.* Ithaca, N.Y.: Cornell University Press, 1964. Computer concordance based on Johnson's 1955 *Poems.* For each word, it provides line-context, line number, first line of the poem, and poem number.

WOODRESS, JAMES. "Emily Dickinson." In *Fifteen American Authors Before 1900: Bibliographic Essays on Research and Criticism,* edited by Robert A. Rees and Earl N. Harbert, pp. 139–68. Madison: University of Wisconsin Press, 1971. Critical and evaluative guide which sorts, ranks, and compares the major scholarship.

2. Biographical Works

BIANCHI, MARTHA DICKINSON. *Emily Dickinson Face to Face: Unpublished Letters with Notes and Reminiscences.* Boston: Houghton Mifflin, 1932. In addition to some letters and poems, the book contains the reminiscences by the poet's niece of life among the Dickinsons.

———. *The Life and Letters of Emily Dickinson.* Boston: Houghton Mifflin, 1924.

BINGHAM, MILLICENT TODD. *Emily Dickinson: A Revelation.* New York: Harper and Brothers, 1954. Examination of Dickinson's later life and of her deep emotional attachment to Judge Otis P. Lord.

———. *Emily Dickinson's Home: Letters of Edward Dickinson and His Family with Documentation and Comment.* New York: Harper and Brothers, 1955. Everyday life in the Dickinson household and in the town of Amherst is described largely through original documents.

CHASE, RICHARD. *Emily Dickinson.* American Men of Letters Series. New York: William Sloane Associates, 1951. Critical and psychological biography stressing close attention to individual poems.

HIGGINS, DAVID. *Portrait of Emily Dickinson: The Poet and Her Prose.* New Brunswick, N.J.: Rutgers University Press, 1967. Biographical portrait of Dickinson; documented largely by a close examination of her correspondence.

JENKINS, MACGREGOR. *Emily Dickinson: Friend and Neighbor.* Boston: Little, Brown, 1939. The author, born across the street from Dickinson in 1869, records memories and impressions of the poet and her family.

JOHNSON, THOMAS H. *Emily Dickinson: An Interpretive Biography.* Cambridge, Mass.: Harvard University Press, 1955. Biographical and critical analysis by the recent chief editor of Dickinson's poetry and letters. Emphasizes the emotional forces in her life with close attention to many poems.

LEYDA, JAY. *The Years and Hours of Emily Dickinson.* New Haven: Yale University Press, 1960. Massive compilation chronologically arranged of biographical materials and documents relating to Dickinson.

POLLITT, JOSEPHINE. *Emily Dickinson: The Human Background of her Poetry.* New York: Harper, 1930. The first full-length biography; notable for advancing the theory of Dickinson's secret love of Major Edward Hunt.

SEWALL, RICHARD B. *The Life of Emily Dickinson.* 2 vols. New York: Farrar, Straus and Giroux, 1974. Most comprehensive biography of Dickinson to date. Includes all the known facts, as well as all the theories, guesses, and legends about the poet, her family, and her surroundings.

TAGGARD, GENEVIEVE. *The Life and Mind of Emily Dickinson.* New York: Alfred A. Knopf, 1930. Early appreciative biography; advances the theory that Dickinson's love of George Gould was forbidden by her father.

WARD, THEODORA. *The Capsule of the Mind: Chapters in the Life of Emily Dickinson.* Cambridge, Mass.: Harvard University Press, 1961. Focuses on Dickinson's inner life at various periods of her development, and on her significant friendships.

WHICHER, GEORGE FRISBIE. *This Was a Poet: A Critical Biography of Emily Dickinson.* New York: Charles Scribner's Sons, 1939. First reliable biography. Treats Dickinson in relation to her New England culture with chapters on her reading, humor, and method.

3. Critical and Interpretative Books

ANDERSON, CHARLES R. *Emily Dickinson's Poetry: Stairway of Surprise.* New York: Holt, Rinehart and Winston, 1960. Very careful, detailed explications of about one hundred of Dickinson's finest poems; arranged thematically.

BINGHAM, MILLICENT TODD. *Ancestors' Brocades: The Literary Debut of Emily Dickinson.* New York: Harper and Brothers, 1945. Daughter of Dickinson's first editor recounts in detail the story of the first editing of the poems; gives attention to family background and the feuds which developed over publication.

BLAKE, CAESAR R., and WELLS, CARLTON F., eds. *The Recognition of Emily Dickinson: Selected Criticism Since 1890.* Ann Arbor: University of Michigan Press, 1964. Collection of some of the best essays on Dickinson that reflect growth of her reputation.

CAPPS, JACK L. *Emily Dickinson's Reading 1836–1886.* Cambridge, Mass.: Harvard University Press, 1966. Thorough analysis of the influence of Dickinson's reading on her poetry.

CODY, JOHN. *After Great Pain: The Inner Life of Emily Dickinson.* Cambridge, Mass.: Harvard University Press, 1971. Psychological study of the poet through insightful analysis of her poems and letters by a practicing psychiatrist.

DAVIS, THOMAS M., ed. *14 by Emily Dickinson.* Chicago: Scott, Foresman, 1964. Useful collection of brief commentaries by noted critics on fourteen of Dickinson's most famous poems.

FRANKLIN, R. W. *The Editing of Emily Dickinson: A Reconsideration.* Madison: University of Wisconsin Press, 1967. Argues for a rearrangement of the accepted chronology of Dickinson's poems as presented in the Johnson edition of 1955.

GELPI, ALBERT J. *Emily Dickinson: The Mind of the Poet.* Cambridge, Mass.: Harvard University Press, 1965. Through numerous passages of letters and poems, this study attempts an internal biography of Dickinson. Discusses her pivotal place in American letters.

GRIFFITH, CLARK. *The Long Shadow: Emily Dickinson's Tragic Poetry.* Princeton, N.J.: Princeton University Press, 1964. Through careful explication of the poems and psychoanalytic interpretations, this study focuses on Dickinson's fears of change, deprivation, commitment, and masculinity.

HEISKANEN-MAKELA, SIRKKA. *In Quest of Truth: Observations on the Development of Emily Dickinson's Poetic Dialectic.* Jyväskylä: Jyväskylän Yliopisto, 1970. Study of Dickinson's stylistic development; focuses on her changing approach to reality.

KHAN, SALAMATULLAH. *Emily Dickinson's Poetry: The Flood Subjects.* New Delhi: Aarti Book Centre, 1969. Insights into Dickinson's major themes from the Indian point of view. Chapters are on nature, love, divine love, death, immortality, and herself.

KHER, INDER NATH. *The Landscape of Absence: Emily Dickinson's Poetry.* New Haven: Yale University Press, 1974. Close, detailed readings of numerous poems as isolated works of art.

LINDBERG-SEYERSTED, BRITA. *The Voice of the Poet: Aspects of Style in the Poetry of Emily Dickinson.* Cambridge, Mass.: Harvard University Press, 1968. Fairly comprehensive examination of Dickinson's poetic language; uses recent linguistic concepts and terminology.

LUBBERS, KLAUS. *Emily Dickinson: The Critical Revolution*. Ann Arbor: University of Michigan Press, 1968. Highly detailed, chronological survey of the growth and development of Dickinson's reputation from 1862 to 1962.

LUCAS, DOLORES DYER. *Emily Dickinson and Riddle*. DeKalb: Northern Illinois University Press, 1969. Combined study of poems, letters, and life; focuses on the cryptic, the questioning, and suggestive elements in Dickinson's poetry.

MACLEISH, ARCHIBALD, BOGAN, LOUISE, and WILBUR, RICHARD. *Emily Dickinson: Three Views*. Amherst, Mass.: Amherst College Press, 1960. Three perceptive essays on Dickinson by three contemporary poets.

MILLER, RUTH. *The Poetry of Emily Dickinson*. Middletown, Conn.: Wesleyan University Press, 1968. Through similarities in imagery and feeling among the poems and letters, this study argues the substance and manner of many of Dickinson's poems grew out of frustrations over publication and unfulfilled love for Samuel Bowles.

MUDGE, JEAN MCCLURE. *Emily Dickinson and the Image of Home*. Amherst: University of Massachusetts Press, 1975. Detailed analysis of home and home life as they affected Dickinson's mind and poetry.

PICKARD, JOHN B. *Emily Dickinson: An Introduction and Interpretation*. American Authors and Critics Series. New York: Barnes and Noble, 1967. General introduction for college students to the poet's life and work.

PORTER, DAVID T. *The Art of Emily Dickinson's Early Poetry*. Cambridge, Mass.: Harvard University Press, 1966. Explores growth of Dickinson's poetic techniques through examination of the poetry before 1862.

SEWALL, RICHARD B., ed. *Emily Dickinson: A Collection of Critical Essays*. Twentieth Century Views. Englewood Cliffs, N.J.: Prentice-Hall, 1963. Useful collection of some of the best essays by twentieth-century critics.

SHERWOOD, WILLIAM R. *Circumference and Circumstance: Stages in the Mind and Art of Emily Dickinson*. New York: Columbia University Press, 1968. Overall study of the development of the mind and poetry of Dickinson; argues that the poet experienced religious conversion in 1862.

TODD, JOHN EMERSON. *Emily Dickinson's Use of the Persona*. The Hague: Mouton, 1973. Thorough analysis of the major personae in four categories of poetry.

WELLS, HENRY W. *Introduction to Emily Dickinson*. Chicago: Hendricks House, 1947. Overall view relating Dickinson's poetry to her personality and to cultural and social environment.

WYLDER, EDITH. *The Last Face: Emily Dickinson's Manuscripts.* Albuquerque: University of New Mexico Press, 1971. This careful study argues that the dashes in the poetry are related to symbols from elocution texts of the nineteenth century, and are meant to affect our reading and understanding of the poems.

4. Critical and Interpretative Articles and Essays

AIKEN, CONRAD. "Emily Dickinson." *Dial* 76 (April, 1924), 301–8. Discusses characteristic themes in Dickinson's poetry; notes Emerson's influence upon her.

ALLEN, GAY WILSON. "Emily Dickinson." In *American Prosody,* New York: American Book Company, 1935. pp. 307–20. Focuses on Dickinson's versification and irregularities; suggests her links with Emerson.

BLACKMUR, RICHARD P. "Emily Dickinson: Notes on Prejudice and Fact." *Southern Review* 3 (Autumn, 1937), 323–47. Critical essay which examines closely Dickinson's language in several poems and dismisses several assumptions about the poet.

FISHER, C. J. "Emily Dickinson as a Latter-Day Metaphysical Poet." *American Transcendental Quarterly* 1 (1969), 77–81. Observes similarities between Dickinson and the seventeenth-century Metaphysical tradition.

HIGGINSON, THOMAS WENTWORTH. "Emily Dickinson's Letters." *Atlantic Monthly* 68 (October, 1891), 444–56. One of Dickinson's most important "Masters" recounts his friendship with her and his earliest impressions of her work.

LOWELL, AMY. "Emily Dickinson." In *Poetry and Poets: Essays.* New York: Houghton Mifflin, 1930. Imagist's evaluation of Dickinson's poetic achievement.

RANSOM, JOHN CROWE. "Emily Dickinson." *Perspectives U. S. A.,* no. 15 (Spring, 1956), 5–20. Broad, appreciative essay; examines "renunciation" in Dickinson's poetry.

SANDEEN, ERNEST. "Delight Deterred by Retrospect: Emily Dickinson's Late Summer Poems." *New England Quarterly* 40 (December, 1967), 483–500. Argues that Dickinson intensified her inner life through disciplined analysis, as seen in a close study of Indian summer poems.

TATE, ALLEN. "Emily Dickinson." In *Collected Essays.* Denver: Swallow Press, 1959, pp. 197–211. Often reprinted essay discusses the historical and cultural environment that produced Dickinson the poet.

THUNDYIL, ZACHARIAS. "Circumstance, Circumference, and Center: Immanence and Transcendence in Emily Dickinson's Poems of Extreme Situations." *Hartford Studies in Literature* 3 (1971), 73–92. Definition and expansion of certain key terms for understanding Dickinson.

WAGGONER, HYATT H. "Emily Dickinson: The Transcendent Self." *Criticism* 7 (Fall, 1965), 297–334. Focuses on Emerson's importance to Dickinson's growth as poet and person.

———. "Proud Ephemeral: Emily Dickinson." In *American Poets: From the Puritans to the Present.* Boston: Houghton Mifflin, 1968, pp. 181–222. Broad essay; treats many important subjects, especially Emerson's influence on Dickinson.

WARREN, AUSTIN. "Emily Dickinson." *Sewanee Review* 65 (Autumn, 1957), 565–86. Wide-ranging essay; discusses biographical and editing problems; considers Dickinson's poems on death.

WILSON, SUZANNE M. "Emily Dickinson and Twentieth Century Poetry of Sensibility." *American Literature* 36 (November, 1964), 349–58. Draws similarities in attitude and technique between Dickinson and modern poets.

WINTERS, YVOR. "Emily Dickinson and the Limits of Judgment." In *Maule's Curse.* Norfolk, Conn.: New Directions, 1938, pp. 149–65. Astute analysis of Dickinson's poetic technique with close readings of several poems.

YETMAN, MICHAEL G. "Emily Dickinson and the English Romantic Tradition." *Texas Studies in Literature and Language* 15 (Spring, 1973), 129–47. Points out similarities in theme, attitude, and technique between Dickinson and the romantics; argues they were a shaping force on her poetry.

Index